GRACE, ORDER,
OPENNESS AND DIVERSITY

D1600290

By the same author:

The Call to Seriousness: The Evangelical Impact on the Victorians
William Morris and His World
The Optimists: Themes and Personalities in Victorian Liberalism
Breaking the Mould? The Birth and Prospects of the Social Democratic Party
The English Middle Classes are Alive and Kicking
The Strange Rebirth of Liberal Britain
Enlightened Entrepreneurs
The Penguin Book of Hymns
God is Green: Christianity and the Environment
O Love that Wilt Not Let Me Go
Marching to the Promised Land: Has the Church a Future?
The Complete Annotated Gilbert and Sullivan
The Celtic Way
The Power of Sacrifice
Columba – Pilgrim and Penitent
Der Keltische Weg
Keltische Spiritualiteit
Abide With Me – The World of Victorian Hymns
Celtic Christianity: Making Myths and Chasing Dreams
The Penguin Book of Carols
Colonies of Heaven: Celtic Models of Ministry and Pastoral Care
Celtic Christianity: Living the Tradition
God Save the Queen: The Spiritual Dimension of Monarchy
You've Got to Have a Dream: The Message of the Musical
Oh Joy! Oh Rapture! The Enduring Phenomenon of Gilbert and Sullivan
The Daily Telegraph Book of Hymns
The Daily Telegraph Book of Carols
Believing in Britain: The Spiritual Identity of Britishness
Pilgrimage: A Cultural and Spiritual Journey
Water Music: Music Making in the Spas of Europe and North America

Grace, Order, Openness and Diversity

Reclaiming Liberal Theology

IAN BRADLEY

continuum

BR
1615
.B73
2010

Published by the Continuum International Publishing Group

The Tower Building   80 Maiden Lane
11 York Road   Suite 704
London SE1 7NX   New York NY 10038

www.continuumbooks.com

Copyright © Ian Bradley, 2010

All rights reserved. No part of this publication may be reproduced or transmitted in any form or by any means, electronic or mechanical, including photocopying, recording or any information storage or retrieval system, without prior permission from the publishers.

First published 2010

British Library Cataloguing-in-Publication Data
A catalogue record for this book is available from the British Library.

ISBN: 978–0–5672–6890–7

Designed and typeset by Kenneth Burnley, Wirral, Cheshire
Printed and bound by MPG Books Group Ltd

The founding fathers of fundamentalism had five principles, so let me match them with a fivefold dedication:

First and foremost, this book is dedicated with profound gratitude to those oases of liberalism where I have found refreshment and encouragement, notably the Iona Community, St Deiniol's Library, Christians Aware, the Free to Believe network of the United Reformed Church, and to fellow liberal believers everywhere.

Second, it is for all who have been at the receiving end of fundamentalist arrogance, bullying and insensitivity.

Third, it is for those on the often difficult faith journey from certainties and fears to doubts and loves. I hope that it may help them to realize that it is worth making and that they are not alone.

Fourth, it is for my many conservative evangelical friends and colleagues, in the hope that they will read to the end, forgive me where they feel that I have erred, and that we may continue to walk, talk, pray and grow together in grace and openness.

Fifth, it is for my son, Andrew, a true liberal who gave me *The Faith of Barack Obama* as a Christmas present with the suggestion that I file it under 'liberal theology'. Perhaps this book will help answer the question as to what his father does actually believe – even if it is in the theological virtues of fuzziness.

Being truly liberal means thinking and speaking in responsibility and openness on all sides, backwards and forwards, towards both past and future, and with what I might call total personal modesty. To be modest is not to be sceptical; it is to see that what one thinks and says also has limits.

Karl Barth

Contents

Preface and Acknowledgements

Between 1910 and 1915 a group of conservative evangelical Christians in the United States, sponsored by two brothers who had made their fortune in the oil industry, published a series of pamphlets on what they called the fundamentals of the faith. Millions of copies were distributed on both sides of the Atlantic promulgating the literal authority and inerrancy of the Bible, creationism and substitutionary atonement. This venture gave birth to a new word in the English language, 'fundamentalism', and inaugurated a century that has seen the steady progress of a narrow, fear-filled, judgemental conservatism not just in Christianity but in the other Abrahamic faiths.

A hundred years on from its birth, we urgently need to escape from the shackles of this modern fundamentalism which has, if anything, increased its grip in the first decade of the twenty-first century. Pastoral considerations, recent biblical scholarship and the urgent need to tackle climate change and avert the so-called 'clash of civilizations' between religions and cultures in an over-populated, globalized world all require a liberal theology of gracious generosity, order, openness and commitment to diversity. I believe that these are also among the chief characteristics of God, as traditionally conceived and worshipped by Christians, Jews, Muslims and other believers.

This book (which is not sponsored from the profits of the oil industry) seeks to expound and recover the basic principles of liberal theology. It is essentially a work of reclamation, springing from a conviction that we need to return to basics (but not, God forbid, to fundamentalism) in our theological understanding in the face of contemporary challenges just as we do in our economic and political understanding. The sacred scriptures and early attitudes and practices of most of the great world religions are often characterized by a broad liberal outlook. It is narrow conservatism that represents innovation and departure from tradition.

The scope and theme of this book have gradually broadened in the years in which I have been working on it. I originally thought of sub-titling it 'Reclaiming Liberal Protestantism' but that seemed too narrow. While the liberal Protestant tradition is certainly a very important part of what I want to reaffirm, there is also a fine tradition of liberal Catholicism, several of whose leading exponents feature prominently in the pages that follow. Then I thought of calling it 'Reclaiming Liberal Christianity', but that also came to feel too narrow. As I have studied the sacred texts of other religions and talked with their practitioners, and especially as I have read and re-read the Koran and talked to Muslims, I have become increasingly persuaded of the existence of a liberal dimension – I am tempted to say a liberal heart – in all the great faith traditions.

This means that while the predominant emphasis of this book is on Christianity, there is a certain amount on other faith traditions, and particularly on Islam and Judaism. Perhaps it is really only the three Abrahamic faiths that can properly be described as having a liberal theology. This is because their monotheism and heavy reliance on sacred texts makes theology, understood as 'God talk', central in a way that it is not true of other faiths, where there is a multiplicity of gods, and written texts do not have quite the same authority. Several of the major themes of theological liberalism, such as contextual and metaphorical rather than literal readings of scripture and emphasizing reason as much as revelation, do not really apply to Hinduism, Buddhism, Taoism, Jainism, Confucianism and Sikhism, which are much less based on the authority of text and revelation. In several respects these other faiths are intrinsically more liberal than the Abrahamic trinity in terms of their pluralism and openness, although they too have spawned their fundamentalists and fanatics.

So it is with a conviction that liberal voices are to be heard and found across all faiths and across all Christian denominations that I offer this manifesto for a reclaimed liberal theology to counter the prevailing and growing conservative fundamentalism of our times. That fundamentalism is to be found in many quarters, most conspicuously and in its most publicized form within Islam as well as among the growing ranks of secular materialists, militant atheists and apostles of political correctness. Within Christianity it is located predominantly in the growing conservative evangelical movement. Because this book is primarily about the Christian context, I will quite often be comparing and contrasting liberal with conservative evangelical theology. I hope that this book will not be read as anti-evangelical, for that is not the message which it is intended to convey. In its original meaning of one who is concerned with proclaiming the good news of the gospel, I consider myself an evangelical. I am also an unrepentant liberal. I firmly believe that there is room for both liberal and conservative theological approaches and that they balance and complement each other. Indeed, I argue in the last chapter that to some extent they reflect different life experiences and personality types and that it sometimes seems as if they are almost genetically conditioned (see pages 158–9). If this is the case, I echo Private Willis in Gilbert and Sullivan's *Iolanthe* (there's my trademark G & S reference out of the way early!) in rejoicing 'that every boy and every girl that's born into this world alive is either a little liberal or else a little conservative', though I do wish that there were a few more little liberals being born nowadays. Liberals need evangelicals to remind them of the reality and power of sin and evil just as evangelicals need liberals to keep bringing them back to the essential goodness of God and of the world that God created.

I have considerable admiration and respect for the evangelical tradition in Christianity, especially in British Christianity. My first book, *The Call to Seriousness,* written 35 years ago and recently republished, chronicles and celebrates the hugely positive influence that evangelicalism had on both public and private life in nineteenth-century Britain.[1] Evangelical Christians were in the vanguard of the movements to abolish the slave trade and slavery, to improve the appalling conditions of factory workers and to clean up political life and reform the institutions of government. I also have a deep and lingering attachment to the revivalist hymns that I was brought up on as a child. However, I am saddened and disturbed at the turn that evangelicalism has taken over recent decades. It has become narrower, more judgemental, more arrogant and more dismissive of the views of liberal believers. This is not just my impression – it is the considered judgement of English evangelicalism's most recent historian, Rob Warner, who notes that 'from the 1920s fundamentalism appears to have had a magnetic effect upon evangelicalism', identifies from the mid-twentieth century onwards 'fundamentalizing tendencies evident in a continuing rightwards drift' and points to the current extremism of what he describes as 'Evangelicalism's Militant Tendency . . . accurately designated, by its exponents and critics alike, as nothing less than unreconstructed fundamentalism.'[2]

I am not seeking to suggest that all evangelicals are fundamentalists – far from it – although I do find it interesting that the two terms are linked in the recent 'Evangelicalism and Fundamentalism in Britain Project', an interdisciplinary research network made up of those of an avowedly evangelical theological persuasion which has explored the intersection of identity between these two positions and the specific question of to what extent Evangelicals in Britain have been Fundamentalists (their capitals, not mine).[3] I am well aware that contemporary evangelicalism is a broad church and that there are increasingly within it those of a generous, open outlook who will feel able to affirm much, if not all, that I put forward in this book, even if they may balk at the label 'liberal' to describe it. Among many in the charismatic and house churches and the so-called emergent church in particular there are stirrings of a new kind of theology which seems to me to be distinctly liberal-leaning and to provide real grounds for hope. However, there is also a growing hard-edged, defensive, fundamentalist mentality to be found among conservative evangelicals, not least within the traditional mainstream denominations. This same mentality is also increasingly to be found within the Roman Catholic Church as well as in Islam and Judaism and in the other major faiths. It is part of the long shadow that fundamentalism has cast over the twentieth century and beyond it and which I believe needs to be countered and challenged, in a spirit of love, humility and grace, by reclaiming the liberal theological tradition.

The fundamentalist founding fathers of 1910 had five principles to which they clung: scriptural inerrancy; creationism as against evolution; substitutionary atonement; the Virgin birth and bodily resurrection of Jesus; and the historical reality of the miracle stories in the Gospels. I believe that the essence of liberal theology can be expressed in four rather broader themes which I believe can also be seen as the key attributes of God: grace, order, openness and diversity. My own

Trinitarian Christian perspective leads me to envisage these themes as belonging respectively to each person of the Trinity and to the Trinitarian Godhead as a whole. I want to propose grace as the particular attribute of God the Father, or Creator; order as the particular attribute of God the Son, or Redeemer; openness as the particular attribute of God the Spirit or Sustainer; and diversity as the attribute of God in Trinity. The three persons of the Trinity are sometimes now referred to as Source, Word and Breath, or as Life-giver, Pain-bearer and Love-maker – formulations which I believe fit well with the categories of grace, order and openness.

These are not exclusive categories. Grace, for example, is clearly an attribute of Jesus whether conceived as Son, Redeemer, Word or Pain-bearer, as well as of God the Father. Nor do the four themes which I am suggesting lie at the heart of liberal theology need to be tied to a Trinitarian framework or understanding for their efficacy. I appreciate that such a framework is not helpful for Muslims or Jews, nor that arguably most liberal of all Christian denominations, the Unitarians. However, I hope that for other Christians, who are likely to make up the majority of readers of this book, it may be suggestive and helpful. For me, the Trinity points to relationship, community and a mutual flow of love and dynamic energy at the heart of the divine in contrast to the authoritarian, despotic, distant image that tends to predominate through concentrating simply on a single father-figure in the sky.

It is no accident that the first letters of these four key attributes spell out the word GOOD. God's goodness is a very liberal theme and one that tends to be downplayed in conservative circles. Conservative evangelical preachers and pastors in my experience speak a lot about God's holiness, awesomeness and judgement but not so much about God's goodness and even less about the goodness of the world that God has created. Proclaiming the intrinsic goodness of God's creation, not least the human part of it, is one of the prime tasks for a new reclaimed liberal theology. Like so much else in liberal theology, it is both highly biblical and highly orthodox, building on the repeated message in the opening chapter of Genesis that at every point in the creation of the world 'God saw that it was good.' It is a key theme of the wisdom literature in the Bible which provides a rich repository of liberal theology: 'You love everything that exists and nothing that you have made disgusts you, since, if you had hated something, you would not have made it' (Wisdom of Solomon, 11.24). This is not to deny the dreadful reality and awful effects of alienation, sin, evil and suffering, but it is to affirm in the words of the Abba song 'I Have a Dream' that helped make the film *Mamma Mia!* break all records: 'I believe in angels – something good in everything I see' (and there's my statutory musicals reference also out of the way early) – which is surely what faith in a creating, loving, life-affirming God calls us to do.

This book is offered as a rallying cry to liberals in all faith communities, and to others who might not immediately or readily identify themselves as such, to rediscover the life-affirming generosity and hope-filled openness which stands at the heart of the liberal tradition in stark contrast to the fear, suspicion and negativity that has been fostered by fundamentalism. In his book, *A Liberal Theology for the 21st Century*, Michael Langford writes, 'a modest assessment of liberal theology is to see it as a tradition of primal importance in the context of open debate or dialogue between people of good will'.[4] It is important to keep that open debate and dialogue going, especially at the present time between Christians and Muslims, and there are plenty of people of good will in both these faith communities. This book is not just for Christians – it is for Muslims, Jews and those of other religions whom I hope it may remind of the liberal heart of their own faith. I hope, too, that it will be read not just by believers but by some of the secularists and atheists who increasingly provide the dominant and not always very liberal ideology among the chattering classes. I echo what a correspondent to the *Guardian* wrote one recent Christmas Eve in response to a characteristic rant against religion in general and Christianity in particular by Polly Toynbee, the high priestess of liberal secular humanism:

> She might reflect that those liberal values she feels passionately about – and has made her career defending – are largely based on Christian principles of forgiveness, compassion and selflessness. Christianity is not the enemy of liberalism as she seems to believe – it is the foundation of it.[5]

Liberal theology is not much in vogue just now. When I first suggested this book to Robin Baird-Smith, the Publishing Director at Continuum, his single-line e-mail response was not encouraging: 'Liberal theology is dead.' I am glad to say that he later recanted and has been immensely supportive, but his initial reaction reflects a widespread feeling on all sides of the theological spectrum. Faced with the rising tide of conservative fundamentalism on one side and an increasingly strident and militant atheism on the other, liberal theology appears stranded and outmoded. It is written off by journalists and academics alike. Andrew Brown, one of the foremost commentators on the contemporary British religious scene, reports 'the slow etiolation of liberal Protestantism'.[6] Gary Dorrien introduces his magisterial and sympathetic three-volume work on the history of liberal theology in the United States with the observation that 'the distinctively liberal tradition of Christian theology is often taken for dead'.[7]

Faced with these and many similar obituaries, it is not an easy time in which to champion liberal faith in either the Church or the academy. It is therefore with particular gratitude that I record my thanks to those havens of liberalism which have sustained me as I have worked on this project. Many of the ideas in this book were first tried out in two summer colloquiums on liberal theology which I co-led at St Deiniol's Library, Hawarden, with the Warden, Peter Francis, in 2007 and 2008. I am hugely grateful to him for his constant support and many insights and to the other participants. I also presented my ideas at a very stimulating conference entitled 'Liberal Voices' organized by the Free to Believe network of the United Reformed Church in October 2008. I am grateful to all those who challenged and supported me there. I first developed some of the material used here in two inter-faith weeks that I led with Caroline Jariwala for the Iona Community at the Macleod Centre on Iona. I thank her and the participants in these weeks who included some wonderfully liberal pastors from the United Church of Christ and the Presbyterian Church of the USA. Those who know my work will not be surprised that the pages that follow are liberally sprinkled with extracts from hymns. I am grateful to Thomas Troeger, Andrew Pratt, Alan Gaunt and Cecily Taylor for letting me reproduce their verses which stand in the great tradition of liberal hymnody. David Simmonds, Ray Simpson and James Gray read and commented helpfully and constructively on some of my draft chapters. I have gained from conversations and e-mail exchanges with Steve Holmes, Martin Camroux and Graham Hellier. Thanks are also due to the evangelical cloud of witnesses by whom I am compassed about both in the Church and the academy – without their stimulation and provocation, this book would never have been written!

This is very much a personal apologia for my faith as it is at this stage on my own pilgrimage. It is being published on my sixtieth birthday. If 60 is in fact the new 40, then it represents the thoughts of one embarking on middle age. If, as I rather fear, 60 is indeed the same old 60 that it always was, then it constitutes the musings of one about to enter the autumn (or, to look on the bright side, the Indian summer) of his life. If it betrays touches here and there of the grumpy old man, there are also, I trust, expressions of the hope that springs eternal in the liberal soul. It represents where I am now. I can only echo Luther and say, 'Here I stand.'

Notes

1. I. Bradley, *The Call to Seriousness: The Evangelical Impact on the Victorians* (London: Jonathan Cape, 1976; new edition, Oxford: Lion Hudson, 2007).
2. Warner 2007, pp. 207, 25, xviii.
3. EFB Project homepage, http://www.eauk.org/efb.
4. Langford 2001, p. 101.
5. Letter from Joe Taylor, *Guardian*, 24 December 2008.
6. A. Brown, 'Religion: The Resurrection', *Guardian*, 2 October 2008.
7. Dorrien 2001, p. xv.

1

Defining Liberal Theology and Charting its History

Liberalism receives a rather good press in the Bible, especially in the Authorized Version. The book of Proverbs promises that 'the liberal soul shall be made fat' (Proverbs 11.25) and Isaiah that when the king reigns in righteousness, 'the vile person shall be no more called liberal, nor the churl said to be bountiful' (Isaiah 32.5). Enlarging on this theme, the prophet observes that 'the instruments of the churl are evil: he deviseth wicked devices to destroy the poor with lying words. But the liberal deviseth liberal things; and by liberal things shall he stand' (Isaiah 32.7–8). The sole reference to liberal practices in the New Testament is also highly positive. Paul tells the Christians in Corinth that they will glorify God by their 'liberal distribution unto all men' (2 Corinthians 9.13).

More modern translations underline that the word 'liberal' is used in these biblical citations to denote generosity, open-heartedness, benevolence and an attitude of blessing rather than cursing others. The New Jerusalem Bible translates the passage in Proverbs: 'The soul who blesses will prosper', while the Revised Standard Version renders Paul's remark to the Corinthians as 'you will glorify God by the generosity of your contribution for others'.

It is significant that this biblical usage defines liberal in terms of a broad, open-minded, gracious, expansive generosity. This is also how the word is principally defined in general dictionaries. The *Oxford English Dictionary*, for example, gives its first modern meaning as 'free in giving, generous, open-hearted, abundant, ample, large'. Yet this is not the principal way in which liberal theology is described in dictionaries of theology where its generosity and broadness are subordinated to a more narrow emphasis on its intellectual and rational aspects. A good case in point is the entry in *A New Dictionary of Christian*

1

Theology by Donald E. Miller, author of *The Case for Liberal Christianity*, which identifies three key characteristics of liberal theology:

1. Its receptiveness to contemporary science, arts and humanities:

    'Liberalism pursues the "the truth" wherever it is found; there is no discontinuity between human truth and the truth of Christianity – hence liberalism shuns compartmentalization as well as the disjuncture between reason and revelation, God and man, learning about oneself or nature and understanding the nature of God. Truth is to be found in experience, guided by reason, more than it is known in tradition or authority. Liberals oppose dogmatism, exclusivism, and appeals to non-verifiable realities. Liberals are open to the truth of other religions. Christianity is not viewed as the only expression of man's search for God or of God's revelation to man. God's revelation of himself is ongoing and present in all places and at all times.'

2. Its sympathy to applying the canons of historiography to the interpretation of sacred scripture. Liberals have traditionally been the most enthusiastic proponents of biblical criticism and contextual readings of scripture:

    'The Bible is seen by liberals as a human document whose primary validity lies in the fact that it records the experience of persons who are open to God's presence. The Bible is not a revealed text, nor is it God's exclusive revelation to humankind. The continual task of the liberal Christian is to interpret the Bible in light of a contemporary world-view and the best of historical research, while at the same time interpreting society from the perspective of the gospel story.'

3. An emphasis on the ethical implications of Christianity: 'Christianity is not a dogma to be believed; it is a way of life, a moral vision to be enacted.'[1]

A more recent definition along similar lines is provided by Gary Dorrien in the introduction to his magisterial three-volume work on the making of the American liberal theological tradition:

> Liberal theology is defined by its openness to the verdicts of modern intellectual inquiry, especially the natural and social sciences; its commitment to the authority of individual reason and experience; its conception of Christianity as an ethical way of life; its favouring of moral concepts of atonement; and its commitment to make Christianity credible and socially relevant to modern people.[2]

These summaries identify several of the key themes of theological liberalism. The receptiveness to contemporary culture is certainly important – liberals are in constant dialogue with science, literature and politics. In Richard Niebuhr's famous analysis, they are placed firmly, and rightly, in the 'Christ of culture' camp.[3] Openness, in all its aspects, is an essential characteristic of liberal theology, embracing as it does the idea of reading the Bible as an open book, a sense of ongoing revelation and an open attitude to other faiths. The emphasis on ethical implications, on faith as a way of life rather than a series of dogmas, has also historically been a hallmark of liberal Christianity. I sense that it may be less of a distinguishing characteristic of liberals now. Over recent decades there has been a much greater engagement with the social gospel and progressive politics on the part of many evangelicals who have been actively involved, including in leadership roles, in justice and peace issues previously thought of largely as the province of the liberally inclined.

A slightly different set of emphases underlies the seven defining characteristics of liberal theology put forward by Michael Langford in his *A Liberal Theology for the Twenty-First Century*:

1. A desire to use rational methods.
2. The wish to take seriously the intellectual climate in which faith has to be lived: 'a faith that encourages one to pursue an open dialogue with contemporary thought, precisely because it is believed that all truth, in the end, will point to God'.
3. Refusal to be overawed by tradition or authority.
4. Dislike of any formal links between Church and state.
5. General scepticism of claims not backed up by appeals to reason or experience.

6. A tolerant attitude towards those who disagree.
7. An emphasis on the importance of the individual that rejects the relevance of distinctions based on nationality, race, religion, social standing and gender.[4]

While Langford rightly emphasizes scepticism and tolerance, he over-states rationalism at the expense of the more emotional elements of feeling and experience which have, at least since Schleiermacher, been at the heart of liberal theology and of its sense of wonder and mystery which I discuss in Chapter 4. The subtitle of his book is 'A Passion for Reason' – I would agree that this is among the passions of the liberal mind but not the only nor even the predominant one.

I would also dissent from his statement that liberals dislike any formal links between Church and state. It is my belief that broad-based established churches, such as we have in the United Kingdom, actually serve liberal Christianity, and indeed the interests of other minority faiths, much better than the system of competitive, free-market religion found in the United States. I do not think it is any coincidence that the ideology of privatization has gone hand in hand with the rise of an increasingly conservative religious fundamentalism. When the *Financial Times* journalist John Lloyd sought my opinion recently as to why Britain has not succumbed to the religious fundamentalism found in the USA, my immediate answer was 'because we have established churches'. It is noticeable that the call to disestablish the Church of England comes predominantly from evangelicals and high church Anglo-Catholics. The supporters of establishment, by contrast, are drawn from the shrinking band of broad church liberals, together with many in the minority faith communities who see the benefits of a broad and hospitable church establishment keeping faith in the public arena.[5]

As I am offering a quartet of liberal values in this book, let me quote a fourth and final definition of liberal theology which comes from a sermon rather than an academic book. It is by Martin Camroux, a minister in the United Reformed Church who has thought much about the liberal theological tradition. Like most ministers, he deals in trinities.

First, the liberal is committed to thinking about faith, to intellectual criticality. Secondly, liberals are committed to the view that no one has the whole truth. Thirdly, liberal faith means the freedom to adapt faith to new knowledge. How can any church be concerned about the truth if it is not willing to do this? What do you do when Galileo shows that the earth goes round the sun or Darwin discovers evolution or biblical scholars demonstrate how the Gospels have come to us? What do you do when it becomes apparent that homosexuality is not a deviant life choice but part of what some people are? The freedom to adapt what one believes as the evidence changes is fundamental to liberalism.[6]

Although Camroux's definition comes closer than the three cited earlier, it still falls short of the sense of liberalism conveyed in the Authorized Version of the Bible. His remarks about homosexuality, like Dorrien's reference to a moral view of atonement, begin to move us from a narrow, rationalistic emphasis towards a more engaged and empathetic human concern. But what is lacking from all these definitions, which come from those who are themselves liberals, is an acknowledgement of the generosity of spirit, the graciousness and the pastoral concern which is surely at the heart of the liberal perspective. Ironically, this element is often more clearly identified by liberalism's critics, as in Mark Elliott's statement of 'Authentic Conservatism': 'Liberal Christianity tends to be refreshing in its generosity of spirit, an ability to affirm the world, which means to affirm life. Liberalism is empathetic.'[7] This is not the only element missing in the four definitions quoted above. They rightly emphasize liberalism's embrace of openness and diversity but they do so in a somewhat over-intellectualized and rationalistic manner and in a way which makes it all too easy for conservative critics and opponents to portray it as weak and pliable, bending with the wind and bowing to every passing new theory and fad. Openness and diversity are undoubtedly key constituents and hallmarks of liberal theology. But so also are grace and order, with their rather different yet complementary emphases – the one on the prevenient pastoral dimension and the other on the importance of balance, structure and restraint. That is partly why they are given pride of place in my liberal quadrilateral.

I suspect that one of the reasons why these and other definitions over-emphasize liberalism's rationalism at the expense of some of its other key characteristics is the widespread belief that liberal theology is a relatively recent phenomenon rooted in post-Enlightenment Continental thought. This permeates much of the recent writing on liberal theology by its supporters. Dorrien, for example, begins his survey of the American liberal theological tradition by observing that 'the idea of liberal theology is nearly three centuries old'.[8] Locating its origins in eighteenth-century Enlightenment thought naturally encourages an emphasis on the rationalism of liberal theology, although it is only fair to point out that Dorrien acknowledges that it was also fed by the well-springs of romanticism.[9] He points to Samuel Taylor Coleridge as the most important influence on American liberal religious thinking, specifically through his insistence in *Aids to Devotion* that religion belongs to the faculty of imagination. The imaginative element is certainly just as important to liberal theology as its rational bias.

In fact, I think we narrow and restrict liberal theology in all sorts of ways, and not just in terms of over-emphasizing its rational character, by seeing it essentially as a product of the eighteenth-century Enlightenment. Undoubtedly some of its distinguishing modern principles were hammered out then. Its origins, however, can be traced much further back, certainly to the sixteenth and seventeenth centuries and in some key respects to much earlier. There is, indeed, a strong case for saying that a broadly liberal outlook distinguished Christian thought in its original and early form and that narrow conservatism constitutes the innovation and departure from tradition. This is true, for example, in respect of the approach to the scriptures. In the early Church and throughout the Middle Ages, the Bible was treated allegorically and broadly seen as a collection of stories, metaphors and models the meaning of which was to be interpreted using the human faculty of imagination. The notion of scriptural literalism and inerrancy is comparatively modern – the product partly of the Reformation's emphasis on *Sola Scriptura* and even more of the pernicious influence of conservative North American Christians in the twentieth century, especially those who promulgated the literal authority and inerrancy of the Bible among the 'fundamentals' of the Christian faith in the 1910s and who established the International Council on Biblical Inerrancy in 1977.

In other doctrinal matters, several of the voices that speak to us most clearly and eloquently from the early Christian centuries have a markedly liberal hue. The insistence of the early apologist, Justin Martyr (c. 100–165), that those who lived before the time of Christ and followed other faiths will be gathered up in the economy of salvation and find their place in heaven and that all who live according to reason are participants in Christ as the eternally existing divine Logos, anticipates much liberal Christian thinking about other faiths and about the importance of reason and order. The Greek father Origen (c. 185–254), often seen as the first systematic theologian, took what would nowadays be described as a historical critical view of the Bible, pointing to its allegorical rather than literal truth, believed in the universal salvation of all humankind, and regarded the prime mission and purpose of the Church as the pursuit of truth and wisdom rather than the salvation of souls from damnation. He resolutely eschewed the notions of penal substitution, propitiation and vicarious atonement which became so dominant in the later medieval Church. In other respects, early Christian beliefs and practices seem to have been markedly more liberal than those in later centuries. There is evidence, for example, that women exercised ministry in the first two centuries of the Church's existence. Constantine's conversion in 313 and the consequent change in Christianity's status to become the favoured religion of the Roman Empire meant that political considerations and power struggles became increasingly important in the Church. The growth of ecclesiastical bureaucracy and rise of sacerdotal and episcopal authority produced a drive for uniformity and a stamping out of perceived heresies. With the fixing of the canon of the New Testament and the promulgation of creeds in the fourth century, a narrow and restrictive orthodoxy triumphed that was very different from the diversity, experimentation and tolerant pluralism of the early Church.

Unmistakeably liberal theological voices continued to be heard throughout the Middle Ages, not least from the British Isles. The British or Irish monk Pelagius (c. 350–418) was repelled by Augustine's teaching of the total depravity of humanity and his concept of original sin as transmitted like a hereditary disease so that even the tiniest baby was utterly evil. He also challenged Augustine's belief in predestination and election and followed Origen in maintaining that God's offer of grace was universal and unconditional. John Scotus Erigena (c. 810–877) sought to counter the damaging dualism which was splitting God away from creation and portraying the physical world as profane. Building on the neo-Platonist writings of Pseudo-Dionysius, he argued that the material world was essentially good and that the natural destiny of all creation was to ascend to God. Seeing theology as a kind of poetry, he further insisted that truth can only be expressed in para-doxes. Peter Abelard (1079–1142) attempted to reconcile faith and reason and championed an exemplary or moral theory of atonement in contrast to the hard-edged judicial theories of propitiation and substi-tution advanced by many of his contemporaries. Abelard envisaged the purpose of Jesus' death on the cross as being the breaking of human hearts rather than the satisfying of an angry God. Seen as a divine action of self-giving love begetting a loving response, the cross was for him much more about moving people to repentance and love than about paying the price for sin. Duns Scotus (1266–1308) also empha-sized the overwhelming character of God's love, revealed in Jesus Christ who would have come into the world even if humanity had not sinned.

There are even glimpses of liberal theology in the art and architecture of medieval churches alongside those frightening frescoes depicting hell, judgement and damnation. The decorations on the Romanesque capitals of the chancel and choir of Cluny Abbey, now re-erected in the old flour store, include not just familiar biblical scenes of Adam and Eve, the trees and rivers of Paradise and the sacrifice of Isaac by Abraham, but depictions of the virtues of faith, hope, charity and justice and of the liberal arts – grammar with a whip, rhetoric in chain-mail armour, dialectic with a book and philosophy holding an open box. They express a theological openness and breadth which is not what we always associate with medieval Christendom.

The Reformation had a double-edged effect on the development of liberal theology, sowing the seeds of modern fundamentalism as well as of modern liberalism. The principle of *Sola Scriptura* championed by the Reformers led directly to the doctrines of literalism and inerrancy at the heart of Christian fundamentalism as it was classically defined in early-twentieth-century United States. A recent study describes evangel-ical Christianity as 'the Reformation's most strident heir in the US and elsewhere'.[10] However, the Reformers also encouraged the development

of liberal thought through their attacks on priestly authority and tradition and their emphasis on the exercise of individual judgement and
conscience. In response to the challenge to Papal authority, people
began demanding the freedom to think critically about their faith.
Perhaps even more importantly, the Reformation restored something of
the pluralism that had existed in early Christianity. A single monolithic
church was replaced by a variety of different denominations. In his
magisterial work on the history of political philosophy, John Rawls
finds the origins of liberalism lying in the initially reluctant acceptance
of the principle of toleration and liberty of conscience that came out of
the Reformation and the religious wars of the sixteenth and seventeenth
centuries.[11] Theological liberalism was also a child of the Reformation
for similar reasons.

An especially distinctive and influential liberal theological tradition
sprang from the English Reformation. The origins of liberal Protestantism are often traced back to the writings of Richard Hooker
(1554–1600) and his promulgation of the Anglican *via media* based
on the equal authority of scripture, reason and tradition. Another key
architect of liberal Anglicanism was Launcelot Andrewes (1555–
1626) whose moderate, eirenic sermons opposed narrow Calvinism
and extolled the virtues of politeness, gentleness, patience, restraint
and good manners. The somewhat neglected group of seventeenth-
century divines led by Benjamin Whichcote (1609–83) and known as
the Cambridge Platonists emphasized divine love over divine justice
and established six principles which remain fundamental to liberal
Protestantism:

1. Christianity is a religion of the heart – true religion is comprised of
   faith in God and love of human beings.
2. Tolerance of other beliefs, far from being a sin, is a Christian duty.
3. The use of reason is paramount in arriving at a knowledge of God
   in contrast to both the 'superstition' of Rome and the 'enthusiasm'
   of Geneva.
4. Christians should have a passion for the unseen along with a delight
   in the seen.
5. Human beings are marked by original righteousness as well as
   original sin.

6. Christian beliefs should be propagated and defended in a gentle and eirenic spirit in contrast to the narrow and bitter partisanship common among many Christians.[12]

Other important progenitors of the liberal Protestant tradition from this period included John Robinson (1575–1625), Separatist pastor to the Pilgrim Fathers, who emphasized the open, continuing nature of God's ongoing revelation (see page 107), and William Chillingworth (1602–44), an Anglican priest who believed that all sincere believers, be they Roman Catholics, Muslims or Socinians, would be saved, and held that 'it cannot consist within the revealed goodness of God to damn him for error that desires and endeavours to find the truth'.[13]

The two most influential liberal thinkers of the seventeenth century, John Milton (1608–74) and John Locke (1632–1704), contributed significantly to both the political and theological dimensions of the Anglo-Saxon liberal tradition and bound them together. Milton stands as the father-figure of the radical English Protestant dissenting tradition with its commitment to liberty, tolerance and open-mindedness. This devout if unorthodox Puritan championed divorce 300 years before it became legal in Britain and in *Areopagitica* (1644) penned one of the most powerful and eloquent apologias ever for religious toleration and the principles of free speech and a free press, valuing 'the liberty to know, to utter and to argue freely according to conscience above all liberties'. He based his argument on the centrality of the Christian concept of free will, the fact that humans are created by God with the freedom to choose between good and ill, which he saw as the greatest gift bestowed by the Creator on his creatures, and the conviction that truth can be arrived at only by the free interplay and exchange of ideas, be they right or wrong.

Recent studies by Joan Bennett and Theo Hobson have located Milton as a radical Christian humanist with a passion for liberty of conscience, and argued that his great poetic works, *Paradise Lost* and *Paradise Regained*, can be read as allegories on the birth of Christian freedom. It is in that they are born free that humans are most obviously made in the image of God – the exercise of freedom is the ultimate theological purpose of human existence and love is the supreme expression of that freedom.[14]

John Locke's contribution was perhaps more to political than theo-logical liberalism, but he stands as one of the great advocates of undog-matic rationalism and as an eloquent opponent of religious fanaticism. His second treatise *Of Civil Government* drew on the idea of the law of God being the law of reason and providing moral guidance. A keen advocate of religious toleration, his *Essay Concerning Toleration* (1667) and later letters on the same subject argued that complete toler-ation should be given to every religious body whose doctrines are neither incompatible with civil society nor require their adherents to give allegiance to a foreign prince. His own religious sympathies were well expressed in the title of one of his major works, *The Reasonable-ness of Christianity* (1695), and conformed with the broad, rational lat-itudinarianism, not given to enthusiasms or extremes, which has been a hallmark of the English and especially of the Anglican religious tem-perament.

While the post-Reformation Scottish theological tradition has often assumed a more dogmatic and conservative tone than the English, it has not been devoid of liberal voices, especially among the so-called Moderate party in the eighteenth-century Church of Scotland. Culti-vated and urbane, the Moderates actively propagated the principles of the Scottish Enlightenment and emphasized the virtues of reason, civilized debate and religious toleration. They were celebrated in verse by Robert Burns who himself was considerably influenced by the moderate minister of the Ayrshire parish in which he grew up:

> O Ayr! my dear, my native ground,
> Within thy presbyterial bound
> A candid lib'ral band is found
>   Of public teachers,
> As men, as Christians too renown'd
>   As manly preachers.[15]

It is significant that Burns associates liberal theology with manliness. This link was cemented in the nineteenth century with the development of Vic-torian muscular Christianity which espoused a liberal theological position alongside its disdain for what it took to be the effeteness and effeminacy of high churchmanship and Catholicism. It is well represented in the writings and career of Thomas Hughes (1822–96), author of *Tom Brown's Schooldays* and pioneer Christian Socialist.

As I have already observed, many recent writers on liberal theology date its origins to the late eighteenth century and see its founding father as the German theologian, Friedrich Schleiermacher (1768–1834). Indeed, some are even more specific and take the publication of his first major work, *On Religion: Speeches to Its Cultured Despisers*, in 1799, as marking the beginnings of liberal theology.[16]

Although I would want to argue for a much older liberal theological tradition, I agree that Schleiermacher was a very significant figure in its evolution. Having had an evangelical conversion experience as a child, he found himself increasingly asking questions about his faith and unable to believe in the idea of Christ dying to placate the wrath of an angry God. Schleiermacher developed two propositions central to liberal theology, first that Christianity is not dependent on any fixed dogma but rather by its nature provisional and open to change, and second that its core is experience of the infinite and a mystery that cannot be fathomed or expressed. Liberal theology undoubtedly experienced its golden age in the nineteenth century and found its outstanding exponents among German academics, rightly described by Dorrien as 'the gods of the liberal tradition'.[17]

German scholars provided one of the most important intellectual bases for the development of modern liberal theology – the school of biblical criticism which treated the Bible like another book, finding within it internal contradictions and emphasizing its context and historicity. Building on these foundations, the two key founding fathers of nineteenth-century liberal Protestantism, Albert Ritschl (1822–89) and Adolf von Harnack (1851–1930), grounded Christianity in the New Testament view of the kingdom of God and emphasized its ethical and moral character. Ritschl saw theology above all as a value judgement in which the good is affirmed and expressed through the principle of God as love with Jesus revealing humanity's true response to unqualified divine grace. Harnack felt that there was an intimate relationship between theology and culture with music, art and literature – for him epitomized in Bach's *St Matthew Passion*, Grünewald's *Isenheim* altar piece and Goethe's *Faust* – communicating the glory of God and showing his purposes. Both men emphasized simple faith in Jesus rather than in the creeds about him, focusing on the historical Jesus as 'the man for others' and the implications of his life and actions for human behaviour.

If German academics supplied modern liberal Protestantism with its foundations of biblical criticism, emphasis on the historical Jesus and a strong ethical imperative, nineteenth-century British thinkers, predominantly clergymen from the established churches of England and Scotland, developed two of its other main themes, synthesis and convergence with the theory of evolution and moral revulsion against theories of penal substitutionary atonement. The controversial Anglican collection, *Essays and Reviews*, which appeared in 1860 and took on board the principles of German biblical criticism, and the important apologetic work, *Can the Old Faith Live with the New?* (1885) by George Matheson, a Church of Scotland minister (1842–1906), argued for the compatibility of Christianity with Darwin's theory of evolution. Another Church of Scotland minister, John MacLeod Campbell (1800–72), restated the doctrine of atonement in a universalist direction, utterly repudiating Calvinist notions of election and the idea of penal substitution. His strong emphasis on the fatherhood of God and headship of Christ was taken up by F. D. Maurice (1805–72), who took much of his own Unitarian upbringing into the Church of England, rejected the idea of eternal punishment and saw the kingdom of God expressed in society, the dignity of humanity and the centrality of sacrifice. Maurice exhibited the deep pastoral strain so characteristic of authentic and gracious liberal Christianity. He once observed that he learned more theology from the wards of Guy's Hospital, London, which he trod as a chaplain, than in his study at nearby King's College. A similarly strong pastoral approach characterized the writings of Charles Gore (1853–1932), the most prominent member of the liberal Anglo-Catholic *Lux Mundi* group, who emphasized the doctrine of *kenosis* and God's laying aside of his omnipotence to become human. A less narrowly theological and more broadly philosophical and political liberalism was championed by T. H. Green (1836–82). Profoundly influenced by German philosophical idealism, he argued that the essence of Christianity is not creeds, dogmatic theology nor the authority of the Church but rather the life of prayer and self-denial and the sacrifice of one's own concerns to a higher ideal.[18]

The United States also had a notable liberal theological tradition in the nineteenth century from which two figures stand out. William Channing (1780–1842), a Congregationalist minister seen as the father of American Unitarianism, attacked the notion of substitutionary atonement and preached the amiable attributes and moral perfection of God and the exemplary way of Christ marked by 'the spirit of love, charity, meekness, forgiveness, liberality and beneficence'.[19] Another Congregational minister, Horace Bushnell (1802–76), built on Coleridge's *Aids to Devotion*, emphasizing the metaphorical nature of religious language and seeing theology as a spiritual art form and a kind of poetry depending on the imagination as much as the intellect. His book *The Vicarious Sacrifice* portrayed Christ's atonement as an illustration of God's eternal principle of love and self-sacrifice rather than a satisfaction or propitiation.[20]

Nineteenth-century liberal Protestantism is often characterized as having three main principles: a commitment to rational argument, debate and analysis; a belief in progress; and a desire to return to the elegant simplicity of the gospel and the teachings of the historical Jesus. Borrowing a phrase also used more specifically to sum up the beliefs of mid-nineteenth-century North American Unitarianism, its central tenets have been presented as 'the fatherhood of God, the brotherhood of man, the leadership of Jesus, salvation by character, and the progress of mankind onward and upward'. While somewhat simplistic and unac-knowledging of the considerable emphasis on the cross and the reality of sacrifice and suffering in the writings of Matheson, Maurice and others, this encapsulation of the nineteenth-century liberal Protestant creed is not wholly inaccurate. It sought the essence of Christianity and found it in the religion *of* Jesus – simple, ethical and practical – rather than the religion *about* Jesus – the Pauline and Hellenist traditions. It emphasized God's goodness and love over God's wrath and tended to view sin more in terms of misunderstanding and dulled spiritual awareness than as radical evil. An exemplarist, moral influence theory of atonement, similar to Abelard's idea of love begetting love, was preferred over the idea of penal substitution, propitiation or satisfaction. Above all, perhaps, as Langdon Gilkey has observed, the most significant achieve-ment of post-Enlightenment Protestant liberalism was to shift the balance between faith and love firmly in favour of the latter. With its demise, the pendulum has swung decisively the other way with the emphasis switched from the exercise of love to defence of the faith.[21]

The dark days of the early twentieth century brought about a reaction against what came increasingly to be seen as the naive optimism of liberal theology. The British Congregationalist theologian, P. T. Forsyth, writing in the middle of the First World War, characterized (or perhaps one should rather say caricatured) it as 'young bustle, good form, gentle faith, genial love, kindly conference and popular publications'.[22] The appalling slaughter of the 1914–18 war led to a widespread loss of faith in the precepts of theological and political liberalism. As Europe and the world plunged into deeper violence, repression and inhumanity through the 1930s, former liberal voices began to question the validity and benignity of the beliefs on which they had been brought up. Richard Niebuhr's searing critique of the liberal faith was not untypical: 'A God without wrath brought men without sin into a kingdom without judgement through the ministrations of a Christ without a Cross.'[23] The times favoured a much more pessimistic and confrontational theological outlook, less gentle and genial. Faith eclipsed love, the holiness and radical otherness of God came to be emphasized much more than God's grace and benevolence, as did the themes of judgement and sin. In the early twentieth century, Karl Barth led a revolt against the comfortable tenets of liberalism and established a new, very different theological approach, still dominant in many theological faculties today, emphasizing divine transcendence, revelation rather than reason and a much harder-aged commitment to orthodoxy.

Not that Barth should be entirely blamed for the de-liberalizing of twentieth-century theology. I recently came across a moving and for me quite unexpected and revelatory remark which he made in the last few months of his life. It contrasts with many of his earlier pronouncements and stands as a wonderful expression of the heart and soul of liberal theology from one not normally numbered among its enthusiasts:

Being truly liberal means thinking and speaking in responsibility and openness on all sides, backwards and forwards, towards both past and future, and with what I might call total personal modesty. To be modest is not to be sceptical; it is to see that what one thinks and says also has limits.[24]

Alas, many of Barth's disciples have not shown this openness and modesty, and since the middle of the twentieth century the prevailing currents of theology have moved in an increasingly narrow, conservative and fundamentalist direction. With notable exceptions like Hans von Balthasar (1905–89), Karl Rahner (1904–84) and Jürgen Moltmann (1926–), most major modern theologians have marginalized culture and expressed theology overwhelmingly in terms of dry epistemology rather than through imagination, historical perspective or pastoral sensitivity and engagement.

Liberal voices went on being raised through the twentieth century, not least in Britain, but they were increasingly crying in the wilderness and being swamped by the swelling tide of conservative orthodoxy. The Anglican priest Alec Vidler (1899–1987) championed liberal theology in the middle decades of the century, defining it in terms of the values of generosity emphasized in the Authorized Version and preferring to talk about 'liberality' in a way that suggested a frame of mind or quality of character rather than a creed or party position. 'By "liberal",' he wrote, 'I mean free from narrow restraint, open-minded and progressive, capable of modification, growth and enrichment. If Christianity has a future before it, it will surely be a Christianity of this kind.'[25] The patron saint of theologians, Vidler suggested in a characteristic piece of eirenic liberal sentiment, should be someone who is tolerant, ready to learn from all people and not only a sinner but a doubter. There were other notable British contributions to popular liberal theology in the 1960s and 1970s. Building on the de-mythologizing work of Rudolf Bultmann, himself the heir to the German biblical critical tradition, Dietrich Bonhoeffer and Paul Tillich, John Robinson, Bishop of Woolwich, produced his best-seller, *Honest to God*, in 1963, and a group of academic theologians published *The Myth of God Incarnate* in 1977. In 1976 the Church of England Doctrine Commission produced a report on the nature of the Christian faith. Chaired by Maurice Wiles, it emphasized the themes of journey, adventure and exploration and made much of the diversity of the Bible. It ended with an essay by Hugh Montefiore about the essential provisionality of Christian dogma and 'the mystery of Jesus being greater than any formulation about him'.[26]

Looking back now, this period seems like something of an Indian summer for liberal theology. The 1980s saw a distinct change of mood and a growing realization on both sides of the Atlantic that liberalism in theology as in politics was under serious threat and in marked retreat. Writing from the USA in 1981, Donald Miller expressed a sense of foreboding:

> As I look to the future, I fear that the middle ground between the non-churchgoing agnostic and the Bible-carrying conservative Christian will be lost. This polarization is unfortunate, because it leaves out the temperate alternative of liberalism, in which one seeks to live within the framework of religious tradition while at the same time interpreting that tradition in terms of a contemporary world view.[27]

From the mid-1980s the tides of both mainstream and academic theology have pulled in a markedly more conservative direction and the terms 'post-liberal' and 'after liberalism' have come into wide usage. Among the first books to use one of these phrases in its title, George Lindbeck's *The Nature of Doctrine: Religion and Theology in a Postliberal Age* (1984) calls for more emphasis on doctrine and on the distinctiveness of Christianity, and a theological approach less open, historically minded, culture friendly, tolerant and ready to receive criticism. In *Theology after Liberalism* (2000) John Webster sees liberalism as a theological movement that has had its day. He portrays it as being associated with late-nineteenth-century German Protestantism and certain strands in twentieth-century British and North American theology, reaching its zenith in the 1960s and 1970s in an ultimately futile attempt to accommodate to modern culture. With Lindbeck and others, he notes approvingly that since the mid-1980s theologians have been much less ready to engage with contemporary culture and present the religious message in intelligible form and much more inclined to emphasize the specificity of Christianity and regard it is as a closed and finished system, not something open and in process. This is certainly true of the approach taken by Stanley Hauerwas' influential *Resident Aliens* (1989) and of what is arguably the dominant tradition in contemporary British academic theology, radical orthodoxy, a strongly conservative movement associated especially with John Milbank,

Catherine Pickstock and Graham Ward which is highly critical of traditional liberal approaches.[28]

Within the mainstream churches in both the United Kingdom and the United States, the last 30 years have seen the steady decline of liberalism and the rapid rise of evangelicalism. In 1986, for the first time more than half of Church of England ordinands were identified as evangelical. Today the proportion is closer to two-thirds, with a substantial part of the remainder belonging to the increasingly conservative Anglo-Catholic wing. David Bebbington, the leading historian of British evangelicalism, confidently predicted in 1989 that it would 'occupy a more salient position within British Christianity within the twenty-first century than in the twentieth', and Alister McGrath wrote in 1994 that 'the future now seems increasingly to belong to evangelicalism, which is coming more and more to constitute the mainstream of American Protestant Christianity'.[29] The death-knell of liberal theology has been sounded from the left as well as from the right. Writing in 1991, Don Cupitt observed, 'In recent years, the liberal creed has been falling article by article.' For him, the only viable options are fundamentalism and post-modern, nihilistic, non-realism where God is simply a human construct. 'Liberalism is being squeezed out, in society, in the church and in the intellectual world.'[30]

The anti-liberal current within the mainstream churches seems if anything to have gathered momentum in the turbulent and troubled opening decade of the twenty-first century, leaving liberals feeling increasingly beleaguered and stranded. The title of a recent book from the publishing arm of the Presbyterian Church of the USA says it all: *Theology for Liberal Presbyterians and Other Endangered Species.* Rob Warner ends his 2007 book on English evangelicalism with the observation that 'the numerical collapse of alternative traditions, Protestant and Catholic, means that any post-secular Christian future will inevitably and perhaps increasingly be shaped by evangelicals'.[31] Writing in the aftermath of the 2008 Lambeth Conference which he sees as a sell-out to homophobia, the liberal commentator Theo Hobson reflects:

It's time to admit that the tradition of liberal Anglicanism is finished. Those Anglicans who carry on calling for an 'inclusive church' are relics of a previous era. They should face the fact that the religious landscape has changed utterly. Liberal Anglicanism has become oxymoronic. For the first time this church has defined itself in opposition to liberalism, taking a decisive reactionary stance on a crucial moral issue.[32]

Within my own denomination, the Church of Scotland, liberal Presbyterianism, or the moderate tradition as it has been particularly labelled in the Kirk, is endangered by the rise of a narrower, more judgemental conservative outlook. Liberal Catholicism is in eclipse as Pope Benedict XVI espouses a notably harder line than his predecessors on Protestantism, inter-faith issues and sexual ethics.

There is a wider global dimension to the current eclipse of liberal Christianity which has essentially been a Western phenomenon associated with the mainstream Protestant churches of Europe and North America. The centre of gravity in Christianity has shifted southwards and eastwards to Africa and Asia. This is re-traditionalizing Christianity and producing an increasingly anti-liberal agenda. The Patriarch of the Russian Orthodox Church talks of liberalism being more corrosive of spiritual values than communism. Within Western Christianity, Pentecostalism and independent evangelical churches are growing while the mainstream Protestant churches continue to decline.

It is not just in Christianity where there has been a significant recent move away from liberalism. It has happened in other religions, most notably in the two other great Abrahamic and monotheistic faiths of Islam and Judaism, both of which have strong and long-standing liberal traditions which are now in eclipse in the face of a rising tide of fundamentalism. The story is much the same as with Christianity – early pluralism and syncretism giving way to narrower and more authoritarian orthodoxy, the emergence of significant reform movements in the nineteenth century and a move towards a much narrower, more conservative and defensive outlook over recent decades.

There is a long-standing liberal tradition in Islam which for more than three centuries has been in tension with the two other dominant traditions, customary Islam and revivalist Islam (also known as Islamism, fundamentalism and Wahhabism). In many respects Islam, like Christianity, was at its most liberal in its earliest days when it had a strongly syncretistic flavour and a clear commitment to *itijihad*, some-times spelled *ijtihad*, the struggle for truth through dialogue, learning and independent reasoning. In this early period Muslims sought wisdom from many sources, not least Syriac Christians, and there was an openness to science, mathematics and philosophy. The ninth-century Muslim prophet, Abu al-Kindi (801–73), declared, 'We should not be ashamed to acknowledge truth from whatever source it comes to us.'[33] As with Christianity, after two or three centuries orthodoxy hardened and religious leaders asserted their authority. By the early twelfth century the door to *itijihad* was closed and Islam had become much more monochrome and antagonistic to debate, with Abu al-Ghazali (1058–1111) teaching that revelation must prevail over reason and predestination over free will.

In his superb sourcebook, *Liberal Islam*, Charles Kurzman charac-terizes liberal Islam, a term which he takes from the Indian legal scholar Asaf Fyzee, as opposition to theocracy, support for democracy, guaran-tees of the rights of women and non-Muslims in Islamic countries, defence of freedom of thought and belief in the potential for human progress. For him this tradition, which has been generally ignored by Western scholars, emerged, like the post-Enlightenment liberal Chris-tian theology associated with Schleiermacher, in the eighteenth century with its founding father being Shah Wali-Allah, the head of a religious seminary in India, who emphasized the power of human reasoning and the cultural contextualization of Islam.[34] The nineteenth century wit-nessed a flowering of liberal Islam with such figures as Jamal al-Din al-Afgani in Iran, Sayyid Ahmad Khan and Ameer Ali in India and Muhammad 'Abduh in Egypt championing *itijihad*, the exercise of independent judgement, against the conservative concept of *taqlid*, or following authority and tradition. They saw the Koran as laying down general principles rather than specific details, and had considerable respect for Western values while insisting that their own liberalism was grounded in the life and teachings of the prophet Muhammad whom they saw as a believer in progress and pioneer of rationalism as well as a strong advocate of free will. Liberal Islam made particular strides in universities and educational institutions. By the early twentieth century liberals were in charge of al-Azhar University in Cairo, Istanbul Univer-sity and other leading schools in the Ottoman Empire, new schools in the Muslim regions of Russia, the Anglo-Oriental college in Aligarh, India, founded by Khan, other universities in South Asia, and the school system in Indonesia.

As with liberal Christianity, liberal Islam reached its apogee in the first two decades of the twentieth century. Ameer Ali's *The Spirit of Islam*, published in 1922 and developed from his *Life and Teachings of Muhammad* (1890) was, in the words of William Montgomery Watt, 'essentially a presentation of Islam and its founder as embodying all the liberal values found in Victorian England'.[35] From the 1920s onwards liberal tendencies in Islam were increasingly challenged and crushed both by secular military might and the new fundamentalism that grew out of the puritanical Wahhabi revival in Saudi Arabia and the *Salafiyyah* movement which sought a return to a perceived pure and primal Islam. Setbacks to secular liberal ideologies in Egypt, the Palestinian crisis and the traditionalist backlash against the secularization of Turkey further contributed to the growth of Muslim fundamentalism in the mid-twentieth century. Faith and certainty were lauded over reasoning and free inquiry as liberal Islam gave way to extreme conservatism and to the secular ideologies of nationalism and socialism. The 1970s saw a brief revival of liberal Islam, notably among Islamic thinkers in the West. Fazlur Rahman, born in Pakistan but based in Chicago, argued in *Islam and Modernity: Transformation of an Intellectual Tradition* (1982) for a new exegesis of the Koran based on the principles of historical criticism and the sense of its overall moral and social objectives. Mohammad Arkoun, Algerian-born Professor of Islamic Thought at the Sorbonne in Paris, called for a new humanism, a much greater intellectual rigour in Islam and an acceptance of multiple interpretations of the Koran and other sacred texts. However, a revival of Islamist extremism and the increasingly unstable atmosphere in the Middle East since the mid-1980s resulted in the violent deaths of several prominent liberals across the Islamic world at the hands of fundamentalists.

As with Christianity, there has been a general sense among Muslim commentators writing over the last two decades that liberal Islam is dead. Aziz Al-Azmeh concluded in 1993 that with the rise of Islamic revivalism, 'the time for Muslim liberalism has certainly passed'. In an article entitled 'The Impossible Life of Moslem Liberalism', Fouad Ajami observes that 'in one Moslem society after another, to write of liberalism . . . is to write obituaries of men who took on impossible odds, and then failed'.[36] The worsening Palestinian crisis, the progress of Wahhabism and the eclipse of the Sufi tradition in Pakistan, the impact of the Iraq War and the 'war on terror' mentality and growing Islamophobia in the West post 9-11 and other terrorist attacks have all served to increase militant fundamentalist tendencies in Islam and weaken any lingering liberal sentiments.

Judaism presents a similar picture. More than adherents to the other two Abrahamic faiths, Jews have always had a liberal and anti-funda-mentalist bias, enjoying wrestling with the difficult texts of the Hebrew Bible, relishing ambiguity and paradox, disputing and arguing with God and having no desire to proselytize or convert others. In the words of Jonathan Sacks, Chief Rabbi of the United Hebrew congregations of the Commonwealth:

> Jews don't read the Bible. We sing it, argue with it, wrestle with it, listen to it, and turn it inside out to find a new insight we have missed before. It is God's invitation to join the conversation between heaven and earth that began on Mount Sinai and has never since ceased.[37]

It seems to me that the origins of liberal Judaism lie in the Rabbinic tradition of imaginative interpretation of the Torah, so different from the literalism of the scribes and Pharisees who so often clashed with Jesus. As with liberal Christianity, however, liberal, or reform Judaism (not always the same thing but the two are usually taken together), is gener-ally given more recent origins and traced back to the the mid-eighteenth century and specifically to the movement of Jews out of their cultural ghettoes to participate in the intellectual life of Enlightenment Europe. Its founding father is usually taken to be Moses Mendelssohn (1729–86) who argued for reason as the basis of Judaism and felt that the key articles of the Jewish faith – belief in the existence of God, the immortal-ity of the soul and divine providence – were shared by all the major reli-gions. As with Christianity, Germans were in the vanguard of liberal movements within Judaism, notably David Friedlander (1756–1834) who held that the Torah contained God's teaching rather than his actual law and that it could be changed to meet a changing world.

Liberal reform Judaism made significant strides in Britain and Germany in the mid-nineteenth century. Claude Montefiore (1858–1938), an English Jew inspired by the broad values of nineteenth-century liberalism, rejected Zionism and the voluntary ghetto of isolation and built on the principles of biblical criticism, attempting to synthesize liberal Christianity and liberal Judaism and create a new purified Judaism which would take over the best of Christian faith.[38] This broad liberal outlook remained the dominant tradition in British and North American Judaism throughout the early decades of the twentieth century. However, understandable reaction to rising tides of anti-Semitism and the horrendous events of the Holocaust produced a hardening of Jewish attitudes and a return to neo-orthodoxy, while the creation of the state of Israel and increasing conflict in the Middle East fuelled a more militant Zionism. Within Europe and the United States, liberal and reform Judaism is now in marked decline, while the more conservative varieties of orthodox Judaism are gaining ground, not least the strictly Orthodox Haredim, literally 'God fearing', who are highly critical of contemporary Western culture and whose growth is likely to make them the largest Jewish grouping in the United Kingdom within a couple of generations.[39]

It is not just within the Abrahamic faiths that liberalism seems to be in marked retreat. Hindu and Sikh fundamentalism is also clearly on the rise, as demonstrated by increasingly militant clashes in India. Overall, it is difficult to avoid the gloomy conclusion of the veteran liberal thinker William Wallace:

Within most organised religions in recent years there has been a revolt against tolerant and liberal interpretations of faith, a fundamentalist reaction that reasserts certainty, making absolutist claims to truth and morality. This is evident in both the Protestant and Catholic traditions of Christianity, as well as within Judaism, Hinduism and Islam. Liberalism as a tradition of toleration and as a set of social and political values, rooted in respect for rational argument, commitment to fundamental rights for all humans, and to communities built upon limited government and a clear division between public and private life, is under attack within its Western heartlands both from the Protestant American Right and from the Vatican.[40]

Notes

1. A. Richardson and J. Bowden, *A New Dictionary of Christian Theology* (London: SCM Press, 1983), pp. 324, 325.
2. Dorrien 2001, p. xxiii.
3. Niebuhr 1951.
4. Langford 2001, pp. 22–3.
5. J. Lloyd, 'Last of the True Believers', *Financial Times Magazine*, 17 December 2005, p. 19. On the liberal argument for established churches, see Bradley 1992 and 2008.
6. M. Camroux, 'What's in a Name – Liberal' (undated manuscript).
7. M. Elliott, 'Authentic Conservatism: Accommodating the Liberal Critique' in Jobling and Markham 2000, p. 45.
8. Dorrien 2001, p. xiii.
9. Dorrien 2001, p. xix.
10. Maroney 2006, p. 14.
11. Rawls 2007, p. 11.
12. See F. W. Powicke, *The Cambridge Platonists* (London: J. M. Dent, 1926) and C. A. Patrides, *The Cambridge Platonists* (Cambridge: Cambridge University Press, 1969). Chapter 5 of Clatworthy 2008 has a good account of what he calls the 'coherentist liberalism' of Hooker and the Cambridge Platonists.
13. Langford 2001, p. 11.
14. Bennett 1989; Hobson 2008.
15. W. E. Henley, *The Complete Writings of Robert Burns* (London: The Waverley Book Co., 1927), Vol. III, p. 65. On the influence of the Moderates on Burns' own religious thought, see R. Crawford, *The Bard: Robert Burns, A Biography* (London: Jonathan Cape, 2009), pp. 30–4.
16. See, for example, the introduction to Chapman 2002.
17. Dorrien 2001, p. xiv. On the importance of the German founding fathers of liberal theology, see F. W. Graf, 'What has London to do with Augsburg?' in Chapman 2002, pp. 18–38.
18. On Green, see Richter 1964; on Macleod Campbell and Matheson, Bradley 1995; and on F. D. Maurice, Young 1992 and Morris 2007.
19. Dorrien 2001, p. 35.
20. Chapter 3 of Dorrien 2001 has a good summary of Bushnell's thought and contribution to American liberal theology.
21. L. Gilkey, 'Plurality and Its Theological Implications' in Hick and Knitter 1988, p. 38.
22. P. T. Forsyth, *The Justification of God* (new edn, Coromandel, Australia: New Creation Publications, 1988), p. 12.
23. H. R. Niebuhr, *The Kingdom of God in America* (Chicago: Willett, Clarke & Co., 1937), p. 173.

24. K. Barth, 'Liberal Theology – An Interview' in *Final Testimonies* (Grand Rapids: Eerdmans, 1977), p. 34.

25. A. Vidler, *A Plain Man's Guide to Christianity: Essays in Liberal Catholicism* (London: William Heinemann, 1936, p. xiii). See also Vidler's *Essays in Liberality* (London: SCM Press, 1957).

26. *Christian Believing: The Nature of the Christian Faith* (London: SPCK, 1976), p. 156.

27. Miller 1981, p. 151.

28. See J. Milbank, *Radical Orthodoxy: A New Theology* (London: Routledge, 1999).

29. D. Bebbington, *Evangelicalism in Modern Britain* (London: Unwin Hyman, 1989), p. 270; A. McGrath, *Evangelicalism and the Future of Christianity* (London: Hodder & Stoughton, 1994), p. 1.

30. Cupitt, 'After Liberalism' in Hardy and Sedgwick 1991, pp. 254, 255.

31. Warner 2007, p. 242.

32. T. Hobson, 'Face to Faith', *Guardian*, 19 January 2008.

33. I owe this quotation to a fascinating article by Graham Hellier, 'Travelling from Chalcedon to Cordoba' in *Signs of the Times* (Newsletter of the Modern Churchpeople's Union, April 2008), pp. 6–7.

34. Kurzman 1998. On the development of liberal thought in Islam see also Gibb 1947 and K. Cragg, *Counsels in Contemporary Islam*.

35. Montgomery Watt 1988, p. 64.

36. A. Al-Azmeh, *Islams and Modernities* (Verso, 1993), p. 33; F. Ajami, 'The Impossible Life of Moslem Liberalism', *New Republic*, 2 June 1986, p. 27.

37. Credo column, *The Times*, 15 June 2002.

38. See M. G. Bowler, *Claude Montefiore and Christianity* (Atlanta: Scholars Press, 1988).

39. On the ideology and growth of the Haredim, see Simon Rocker's 'Face to Faith' column, *Guardian*, 7 March 2009.

40. W. Wallace, *Meeting the Challenge* (13 September 2005), p. 3, from http://www.meetingthechallenge.net, accessed from internet 11/10/2005.

2

The Present Predicament and the
Challenge to the Liberal Frame of Mind

Liberalism, in all its manifestations, is as much a frame of mind as a coherent philosophy. Before embarking on the task of reclaiming liberal theology that will occupy the rest of this book, it is worth pausing to reflect on why liberalism generally is presently at such a low ebb and where the main challenges to it are coming from. Fear is the biggest enemy to liberal values because fear breeds fundamentalism. In the words of Imam Muhammed Ashafa, who works with his former sworn enemy Pastor James Wuye to bring reconciliation and healing between Muslims and Christians in Nigeria: 'The greatest obstacle to liberal theology is fear of the unknown and fear of the enemy.'[1] In his excellent book on the subject, Malise Ruthven portrays fundamentalism as a response to pluralism and the fact that globalization has brought religions into daily contact with their competitors, leading to a demonizing of the other.[2] Writing about 'the politics of horror in Conservative Evangelicalism', Jason Bivins describes the increasingly dominant strain in North American Christianity as 'the religion of fear' driven by a conviction that the United States is being taken over by atheists, liberals, feminists and gays.[3]

Just as fear breeds fundamentalism, so uncertainty encourages conservatism. We are living through very uncertain times and it is not surprising that they have produced within Christianity, as within other faiths, a resurgent ultra-conservativism which craves certainty and sees everything in terms of black and white. This new and growing form of fundamentalism has five major characteristics:

1. It tends to be judgemental and unforgiving rather than gracious and generous.
2. It is closed rather than open, claiming to know all the answers,

seeing no need to look outside its own narrow confines and regarding those beyond them as heretical.

3. It is uniform and monochrome with little time for diversity, difference, discussion or debate.

4. It focuses on human depravity rather than human or divine goodness and tends to castigate rather than affirm.

5. It often adopts a fearful siege mentality and tends towards the apocalyptic.

This profoundly illiberal ultra-conservative Christianity has its home and base in the United States. Polls suggest that the proportion of North Americans describing themselves as evangelicals has doubled over the last 50 years, from 18 per cent in 1960 to 36 per cent in 2010. The rise of the religious right in the United States has been chronicled in several recent studies, perhaps most frighteningly in all its hysterical, end-times millennarianism by John Gray in *Black Mass: Apocalyptic Religion and the Death of Utopia*.[4] I am all too conscious of the temptation to engage in what has become an increasingly popular pastime in Europe, baiting those on the other side of the Atlantic and indulging in anti-American prejudice. Some of the most liberal Christians that I have encountered come from the mainstream denominations in the United States, notably the Presbyterian Church of the USA and the United Church of Christ. However, I also have to say that North American Christians have also displayed some of the narrowest and most bigoted conservatism that I have ever experienced. It is particularly in the United States that the retreat from reason that characterizes Western culture in general and conservative fundamentalism in particular seems so marked, as evidenced in the galloping progress of creationism and the obsession with Armageddon. I am worried about the growing American influence on both the Church and the theological academy in Britain, coming both directly from the rising number of very conservative pastors, lecturers and students who are coming over here, and indirectly from the increasing dominance of North American theological and ecclesiological publications, resources and attitudes in British churches and theological colleges. Interestingly, Alec Vidler expressed very similar qualms more than 60 years ago, after a three-month visit to the USA in 1947. He summed up his experiences in a chapter of his book *Essays in Liberality* entitled 'The Appalling Religiousness of America'.

I am not alone in having a sense of unease about the Americanization of British churches. The recently published posthumous autobiography of G. B. G. McConnell, a minister in the Presbyterian Church of Ireland, deplores the increasingly narrow and strident conservative evangelicalism in the church in which he grew up and served throughout his life. He blames it on the influence of what he calls 'the resurgence of fundamentalism under the guise of evangelicalism in North America' and notes:

In Northern Ireland one gets the impression that in recent years the evangelicals whose theological nourishment comes mostly from this side of the Atlantic have changed considerably; but those whose closest links are with American fundamentalism have tended to remain in the hard and narrow channel with which we are all familiar.[5]

McConnell points to another factor at work in the current ascendancy of conservative evangelicalism, the tendency of liberals to be supine in crucial church debates and let the conservatives dictate the agenda. Writing about his own church's General Assembly, he notes that

the forces of reaction are usually well organised when it comes to vital debates, while too often those who take a more liberal view are absent, either because they are away attending to their parochial work or simply because they have not been alerted to their duty . . . The result of all this is that, increasingly, decisions are made which do not, I feel, really represent the bulk of our membership.[6]

This phenomenon will be familiar to many in the main denominations.

In his recent book *Liberal Faith in a Divided Church*, Jonathan Clatworthy points to a similar state of affairs in the Church of England where the conservatives make all the running in major debates and the bishops always give in to them and never to liberals. This is because if they look like disappointing the conservatives, the bishops are threatened with a split or schism in the church. Offended liberals, on the other hand, will not leave the church but will carry on supporting it, albeit a little more grudgingly.[7] Conservatives are much better at organizing, setting up pressure groups and fighting their cause than liberals who are instinctively uneasy about creating factions and picking a fight. Conservatives are also more enthusiastic about issuing manifestos and rallying cries, a recent example being the declaration establishing a fellowship of confessing Anglicans (FOCA) on the basis of a fourteen-point declaration following the Global Anglican Future Conference in Jerusalem in June 2008, a checklist of conservative theological principles which included the inerrancy and sufficiency of scripture, the unique and universal lordship of Jesus Christ and the unchangeable standard of Christian marriage as the only proper place for sexual intimacy.

It is particularly over the issue of homosexuality that the new Christian right has made the running and dictated the agenda, reversing the broad, fuzzy, generally tolerant and pastorally sensitive consensus that has hitherto predominated in the mainstream churches and creating much more polarization and division. It is the battleground on which conservative evangelicals have chosen to pick a fight and flex their muscles, and they have largely triumphed. Thanks to the obsession of the media with this issue, the conservatives' victory has been most publicly displayed in the Anglican communion and especially in the Church of England which has traditionally taken a broadly liberal line on same-sex relations. Anglican bishops were, indeed, in the vanguard of the movement to decriminalize homosexuality in the 1960s, arguing that society had no right to concern itself with what consenting adults do in private. With the rise of the new militant conservative evangelicalism which regards homosexuality as a sin and seeks to rid the church of gay clergy, the mood has changed. The 1998 and 2008 Lambeth Conferences, which brought bishops of the Anglican communion together, saw liberalism in retreat and in the eyes of many marked a victory for homophobia and reaction. A resolution passed by the 1998 conference rejected homosexual practice as 'incompatible with Scripture'. The Windsor Report of 2004, produced by a Commission set up under Archbishop Robin Eames, basically sided with the conservatives' position.[8]

The way in which conservatives have picked the issue of homosexuality and used it to alter the whole character of a mainstream church is well illustrated in what has happened within my own denomination over the blessing of civil partnerships. Traditionally, ministers in the Church of Scotland have been allowed to exercise freedom of conscience on sensitive pastoral matters. With the legalizing of civil partnerships between same-sex couples, ministers found themselves being asked to bless Christian couples who had entered such partnerships as a commitment to and expression of faithful love. Instead of respecting the traditional practices of the church and leaving it to the consciences of individual ministers, conservative evangelicals in the Kirk, mobilized under the umbrella of 'Forward Together', pressed for a formal ruling on whether blessings of civil partnerships should be given. The church's legal affairs committee ruled very properly that in accordance with the law and traditions of the Church of Scotland, this was a matter for the consciences and pastoral sensitivities of individual ministers. Those who felt it right to bless a civil partnership of a faithful and committed same-sex couple should be free to do so without censure. Those ministers whose consciences and theological position did not allow them to bless a same-sex relationship should be similarly free not to.

This sensible and sensitive ruling was not acceptable to the conservatives. 'Forward Together' brought to the church's 2006 General Assembly a motion to make it illegal for any minister to bless a civil partnership. After a measured and serious debate, it was rejected on the floor of the Assembly by a narrow majority. Not content with this, the conservatives invoked a procedural device allowing contentious issues to be voted on at Presbytery level. The presbytery vote went 36 to 9 in favour of outlawing blessings of civil partnerships, an apparently convincing grass-roots victory for the conservatives. In fact, the total number of votes cast in the presbyteries produced a more even split – 1,563 in favour of the conservatives' innovation and 1,007 in favour of maintaining the *status quo*. A clear majority of members of the big urban presbyteries voted for keeping the principle of ministerial discretion and freedom of conscience but they were outvoted by those in the smaller rural and Highland presbyteries who supported the conservative position. As a result there is now a situation where ministers can be disciplined for following their consciences and their pastoral instincts and blessing a faithful, stable, loving relationship. A narrow uniformity based on the theological position of one particular tradition has been imposed on what has always been a broad and diverse church, encompassing both liberals and conservatives.

The sense both of regret and foreboding felt by liberal ministers in the Church of Scotland as a result of this abandonment of one of its most cherished principles is eloquently expressed by John Owain Jones, a parish minister of over 25 years' standing who feels called by his own conscience and his theological understanding that where love is, there is God, to bless gay Christian couples in loving, disciplined, faithful relationships:

> Up to now, I have been allowed actually to espouse, actually to believe, the reverently critical view of Scripture I was taught at university and which has fed and nourished my faith. Just as they [the conservatives] have been allowed to reject it.
>
> Ministers have had this freedom of conscience – they as much as I. We belong to different communities within the society of the Church of Scotland. We work out our theologies in different shared contexts. But the real difference, I fear, is that they feel that the Church of Scotland should be[come] a community which functions exclusively on their values, their understandings. I want a law that safeguards their conscience as much as it does mine. I want the Kirk to be a liberal church, with space for them and for me. I want the Kirk to be a 'society of communities' which is what it already is. I worry that they do not see the Kirk this way and that they do not have a place for me in the Church.[9]

These recent events within my own church highlight a profound and, for liberals, very worrying trend within the mainstream Protestant churches. Evangelical-led assaults on traditional pastoral practices have forced issues and defined boundaries in rigid black and white terms, leaving little if any room for different interpretations and pastoral discretion. They have also resulted in the creation of a much more polarized, partisan and faction-ridden atmosphere within churches that have traditionally been broad, inclusive and diverse. Conservative evangelicals cannot be entirely blamed for this increasingly polarized atmosphere – within the Church of England, Anglo-Catholics associated with the 'Forward in Faith' movement have also become noticeably more assertive and combative. Anglicanism has always prided itself on its broad inclusivity and ability to hold together those of very different theological persuasions and styles of churchmanship in reasonable harmony. That very liberal ethos is now under severe strain, with the various factions becoming much more aggressive and less respectful of each other's positions and traditions. Other traditionally broad churches, like the Church of Scotland, which have hitherto been largely free of partisan pressure groups and organized factions, now find themselves pitched into this unhappy state of division because of conservative evangelical determination to enforce a particular party line. This new trend towards factionalism and in-fighting within churches which have traditionally valued their inclusivity and breadth is particularly hard for liberals who are naturally eirenic and conciliatory and often feel uneasy about setting up or joining party groups, still less organizing themselves for conflict.

For liberals, a disturbing aspect of this increasingly partisan and confrontational atmosphere in churches is that the battle lines are often drawn up according to age, with youth on the side of the conservative forces. In the most heated debates in my own church over the last twenty years, on ecumenical relations, gay ministers and the blessing of civil partnerships, the liberal voices have largely been those of the over-50s and the conservative position has been most clearly and consistently articulated by those under 45, especially by young male ministers. Gatherings of liberal groups like Free to Believe and the Progressive Christianity Network are largely made up of the late middle-aged and retired. Conservative evangelical pressure groups, by contrast, have a high proportion of young members, notably again relatively recently ordained male clergy. Within my own denomination, the conservative drift within the ministry has recently received a significant boost from a change of policy over ordination training. Historically Church of Scotland clergy have been trained by taking a theology degree in one of the four ancient Scottish university faculties of divinity, thus ensuring a broad, intellectual grounding. Since 2006, in response to evangelical lobbying, the Highland Theological College, avowedly conservative evangelical in its ethos, has also been recognized and approved by the church for ministerial training. Glasgow International Christian College, a former Bible college, is likely soon to be accorded similar recognition, and there is even a possibility that the university faculties might no longer be used for training ministers. A church which has always prided itself on giving its clergy a broad, liberal education in institutions where they mix with those of different theological perspectives and of no faith, is switching to training ministers in colleges where the teachers and fellow students come from one single narrow theological tradition.

In fact, increasing conservatism among both students and teaching staff is making traditional British university theology faculties more and more like Bible colleges in both ethos and outlook. This is partly a result of the American influences noted above and also a reflection of the general and in many ways understandable craving for certainty among young people growing up in a frightening world. One of its clearest manifestations is the disappearance of the Student Christian Movement (SCM) from many university campuses, leaving Christian Unions (CUs) as the only representatives of Protestant Christianity. The SCM was for long the torch-bearer of liberal Protestantism. Its cata-strophic decline since its 'golden age' of 1945–65 clearly mirrors the broader collapse of liberal theology and its waning appeal to students and intellectuals.[10] CUs, by contrast, are flourishing and are often among the largest student societies on campus. Firmly committed to conservative evangelical doctrinal principles, many are adopting an increasingly exclusivist mentality in keeping with the general spirit of the times. A recent study attributes the growth of CU-style conservative evangelicalism in British universities to the rise in student numbers over recent decades and the increasingly liminal experience of university life for many young people moving away from home and finding group identity and community among like-minded peers through adopting a narrow and rigorist Christianity in marked contrast to the ethical norms of the wider student body.[11] Roman Catholic student groups have also moved sharply to the right, adopting an increasingly hard line and anti-modernist stance.

The increasing theological conservatism on the part of students is mirrored among academics. A survey undertaken in 2001 by David Ford, Professor of Theology at Cambridge, of the state of theology in British universities, revealed the almost complete disappearance of the eirenic, broad church liberal strain prominent for so long especially in Anglican dominated institutions. I myself have argued that this is not just an aspect of the general collapse of liberal values in the face of the rising conservative evangelical tide, but also in large part a consequence of the displacement of history by philosophy as the principal academic handmaiden to theology. Historical theology, more than systematic or philosophical theology, has always had a strong pastoral and practical concern and a distinctively liberal hue. John Webster rightly identifies as one of the main characteristics of post-liberal theology that it is much less historically minded and engages much more with philosophy than the old liberal theology. One might imagine that a mind trained and steeped in history would incline towards conservativism, but more often than not it is profoundly liberal. William Ewart Gladstone is a supreme case in point, his strongly and increasingly liberal stance on political, religious and social issues being informed and moulded by his historical reading and imagination. History, perhaps because it deals with real people, their hopes and aspirations as well as their crimes and follies, rather than with abstract concepts and theories, tends, like experience, to have a humanizing and temporizing effect. Karl Barth was absolutely right to say that being truly liberal means being open to the past as well as to the future. Church historians, in my experience, are much more likely to be liberal in their outlook than systematic and philosophical theologians. Divorcing academic theology from history and making it ever more philosophical has rendered it more dogmatic, harder-edged and less pastoral. A key element in any reclamation of liberal theology must be the promotion of historical awareness which, with its sense of the importance of context and change, is the antithesis of fundamentalism and literalism.[12]

A greater sense of history and the breadth and generosity of spirit that goes with it would also help rescue liberal theology from the somewhat strident and obscure byways into which it has been diverted in recent decades. Theologies driven by and focused on the agendas of feminism, liberation, queer theory and post-modern relativism, however liberal in intention, have all too often been detached from the

life of the churches and the believing majority and pursued predominantly in narrow academic circles. They have pushed progressive
theology in an increasingly partisan and recondite direction and
provoked a conservative backlash and the assertion of a new and
equally narrow neo-orthodoxy in response.

Theology is not the only academic discipline that has moved in a
narrower, more conservative direction in recent decades. The tyranny
of specialization, encouraged by government-led initiatives like the
research assessment exercise, has meant a retreat from breadth,
teaching and learning and a concentration on ever narrower research.
In Britain, at both university and school level, liberal education as it has
traditionally been understood is under assault. The very first definition
of liberal in the *Oxford English Dictionary* is 'of those arts or sciences
that were "worthy of a free man", opposite to servile or mechanical.
Later of conditions, pursuits, etc. "becoming of a gentleman"'. It goes
on to say that this essentially historical definition is 'now rare' except of
education. Sadly it is all too rare even there now, having been all but
destroyed by an academic culture which values depth over breadth,
research over teaching and audited outcomes over learning. The
plaudits, the prizes and the promotion in universities go to those academics who spend their time researching in ever narrower areas and
writing articles in learned journals which – and this seems almost a
matter of congratulation – will be read by one or two people who
happen to share the same specialist interest. Writing for a more general
readership, teaching and pastoral concern for students count for little.
In schools, liberal education is being driven out by the relentless toll of
testing, auditing and examining and the ever more centralized control
and constriction of the curriculum. This fundamentally illiberal trend is
not just confined to education, of course, although it is doing particular
damage there. Discussing the relevance today of the classic liberalism of
J. S. Mill, John Skorupski rightly asks: 'Is the economic and intellectual
specialisation that modern society absolutely requires reconcilable with
the liberal ideal of harmonious all-round development?'[13]

The slow, steady erosion of mainstream Protestantism and its distinctive ethic has also had a deleterious effect on the liberal frame of
mind. Protestantism has certainly had its share of bigotry and fundamentalism and it spawned that dour, dull philistinism that Matthew

Arnold attacked in *Culture and Anarchy*. However, it also encouraged a culture of hard work, high literacy, self-discipline, social responsibility, democracy and independent thought. Protestantism helped to create the conditions for the Enlightenment. The strenuous, high-minded, fiercely independent frame of mind characterized as the Protestant ethic has been an important contributor to liberalism, not least in giving it moral backbone and keeping it from a flaccid, self-indulgent libertarianism. The Protestant ethic encouraged Christian engagement in progressive causes. This produced a confluence between liberal theology and liberal politics, epitomized in the career of David Steel, son of a Church of Scotland minister standing very much in the Kirk's moderate tradition. Looking back on a career which saw him rise to the leadership of the Liberal Party, he has written about his father: 'I came to realize that, unconsciously, his influence on my political direction had been immense, and my activity in the anti-apartheid movement, abortion law reform, Scottish self-government and international development were all inspired by his background and example.'[14]

This Christian commitment to progressive political and social causes has not disappeared. To some extent, indeed, it has passed to and been taken up by evangelicals who are increasingly engaging with social, economic and political issues.

But something very distinctive to the liberal ethos has been lost with the virtual collapse of liberal Protestantism. It is that strenuous high-minded ethic associated with the phrase 'the Nonconformist conscience' that had such a major impact on philanthropy and progressive politics in the later nineteenth and early twentieth centuries. The denominations which exemplified that conscience and which nursed liberal Protestantism, Unitarianism, Presbyterianism and Congregationalism, in particular, appear now to be in meltdown in the United Kingdom and in serious decline in the United States of America.

The challenge to liberal values is not just coming from the theological and political right. It is also coming from the rise of militant secularism, which in its own way can be almost as fundamentalist as ultra-conservative Christianity or Islam. Radical post-liberal non-realists who deny the existence of God in any real sense make it easier for conservative evangelicals to brand liberals as essentially non-believers. Like many liberals that I know, I myself believe in and worship an objective personal deity.

I accept that there are other ways of expressing the ultimately unknowable mystery of God – Paul Tillich's concept of the ground or depth of all being is one – and I am reluctant to exclude any genuine spiritual seekers from the liberal fold. However, I agree with Jonathan Clatworthy when he says:

> The assertion that there is no God does not in itself seem to me to merit the title of religious liberalism, any more than anarchists are political liberals or opponents of capitalism are economic liberals. I do not share the view – common among religious conservatives – that liberals are, so to speak, half way between conservatives and non-believers. It is indeed true that liberal religious communities tend to be more sympathetic to non-believers than conservative religious communities are; but that is because they are more sympathetic in general to people who do not share their views. The religious beliefs of liberals are at least as strong as those of conservatives.[15]

The contemporary culture of political correctness has its own tendency towards judgementalism and narrow conformity and is in its way just as inimical to liberal values as is conservative evangelicalism. It, too, wants everything clear-cut and spelled out in black and white with nothing left vague, muddled or fuzzy. Ambiguity and blurred edges, territory which liberals often find themselves inhabiting, are equally unappealing to the militant secularist, the strident campaigner for political correctness and the conservative fundamentalist. A key part of the reclamation of liberal theology will, I believe, involve the rediscovery of the virtues and advantages of fuzziness – a profoundly counter-cultural enterprise in the current climate.

Liberal values are clearly threatened by the meaner, narrower, less generous spirit which undoubtedly exists throughout contemporary society as a result of social and cultural changes and is epitomized by the emphasis on rights to the exclusion of responsibilities and obligations. This is particularly evident within the established churches of England and Scotland which are in danger of succumbing to a narrow congregationalism and sectarian mentality. An increasing number of clergy are less and less interested in parish ministry and providing the ordinances of religion to the unchurched majority through the occasional offices of parish baptisms, marriages and funerals, and ever more narrowly focused on ministering to gathered congregations of the committed. There are understandable reasons for this shift of perspective away from broad church inclusivity in terms of increasing pressure on time and human resources, but it is also symptomatic of a wider shift of attitudes throughout society away from liberal generosity and graciousness towards more selfishness and laziness.

Perhaps the most serious challenge to the liberal mind comes from the increasingly brutalized and suspicion-laden tenor of our culture, institutions and public discourse. In large part because of the influence of the media and the pressures of rampant materialism, there is a general retreat from those values of graciousness, urbaneness, politeness and generosity that the Authorized Version defines as the essence of liberalism. We are undoubtedly becoming a more self-centred and more boorish society driven increasingly by the principle of 'me first'. A culture of over-regulation driven by fear and suspicion has replaced a climate of trust and open engagement with other people. The proportion of British adults who trust each other has halved over the last 40 years from 56 per cent to 29 per cent. As a result, and thanks also to the impact of new technologies, rule-bound, box-ticking, risk-averse procedures are increasingly replacing direct human contact and initiative. It is hard for liberal voices to be heard in this climate, still less for liberal values to prevail. It is against this bleak background, but with a recognition that there are hopeful signs of change and a conviction that, by the grace of God, the tide will and must turn, that I now embark on the task of reclaiming liberal theology not out of sentimental attachment to an outworn creed but because I believe that it is sorely needed in our present predicament.

Notes

1. Speech at Scottish Inter-Faith Day, St Andrew's, 30 November 2008.
2. Ruthven 2004.
3. Bivins 2008.
4. London: Allen Lane, 2007.
5. McConnell 2001, p. 39.
6. McConnell 2001, p. 88.

7. Clatworthy 2008, p. 7.
8. 'Saving the Soul of Anglicanism', 2008 Conference report of Modern Churchpeople's Union. See also Clatworthy 2008 and in P. Francis (ed.), *Rebuilding Communion: Who Pays the Price?* (Hawarden: Monad Press, 2008). See also S. Bates, *A Church at War* (London: I. B. Tauris, 2004).
9. J .O. Jones, 'The Tip of the Iceberg. Is it Really Just About Civil Partnerships?', *One Kirk* website.
10. Boyd 2007.
11. E. Dutton, *Meeting Jesus at University: Rites of Passage and Student Evangelicals* (Aldershot: Ashgate, 2009).
12. I. Bradley, *Back to the Future: A Sense of History and the Liberal Mind* (Hawarden: Monad Press, 2001).
13. Skorupski 2006, p. 98.
14. *Church Times*, 13 July 2007, p. 17.
15. Clatworthy 2008, p. 15.

3

Grace

Grace is the prime attribute with which God is associated in the sacred texts of the world's three major monotheistic religions. The Lord's gracious and merciful nature is constantly reiterated in the Psalms, the hymnbook of the Jewish people. The phrase 'the grace of God' occurs 26 times in the Christian New Testament, where it is especially put on the lips of the apostle Paul. In his farewell speech to the Christians of Ephesus, Paul says that the whole purpose of his ministry, indeed of his life, is 'to testify to the gospel of the grace of God' (Acts 20.24). Every *sura* or chapter of the Koran but one begins 'in the name of Allah, the compassionate, the merciful'.

Grace is also a key theme in liberal theology. Liberals emphasize God's open, generous, perpetually forgiving nature while not ignoring themes of judgement and righteous indignation which are also present in the scriptures. At its best, when it is being true to its nature and its calling, liberal theology itself expresses an essential graciousness recognized by its critics as much as by its proponents (see Mark Elliott's comment on page 5).

This chapter explores the concept of grace as it is applied to God, as it has been understood in the liberal theological tradition and as it might inform and inspire a new liberal theology. First, it is important to define the term. The word 'grace' is less commonly used now than it once was – an indication is its almost complete disappearance as a girl's name. Few Christians now regularly say 'Grace' at the beginning of a meal, though most still conclude a service or meeting by invoking: 'the grace of our Lord Jesus Christ, the love of God and the Fellowship of the Holy Spirit', a phrase first found in 2 Corinthians 13.14. The Greek word used in this and other New Testament passages, καρις, carries a multitude of English meanings including grace, kindness, mercy,

goodwill, a favour, gift, blessing, thanks, gratitude, graciousness, pleas-
antness or a special manifestation of divine presence, activity, power or
glory. Among the dictionary definitions of the English word 'grace' are
attractiveness, charm, becomingness, kindness, courtesy, mercy, favour
and blessing. This breadth of meaning is important and appropriate
because it points to the breadth of God.

To emphasize the primacy of grace among God's attributes is to
affirm that the world was created and is sustained out of love and generosity. It establishes important truths about our existence and our relationship with our creator. We are here not as the result of some neutral
or arbitrary experiment but because someone wanted us to be. God did
not create the universe like a scientist in a laboratory but as a parent
giving birth to a child. It is significant that the Hebrew and Arab words
often translated as grace or mercy both derive from the root *rahm*
which means womb. This connection between grace and creation is
fundamental. As *The Oxford Companion to Christian Thought*
observes: 'in the Christian tradition "grace" sums up the relationship of
the Triune God with creation. It depicts this relationship as grounded in
the freedom of God's love and as directed towards the perfecting of
God's communion with creation'.[1] This quotation underlines the close
relationship between grace and freedom. Not only does grace give God
the freedom to create gratuitously, it gives us as creatures the freedom
to choose and follow our own lifestyles, including the freedom to go
astray and to fail. A creator without this central attribute of grace
would have simply demanded love and obedience. Alan Gaunt
expresses this well in one of his hymns:

> What but your holy love's stupendous grace,
> Which knew the outcome, could have left us free in disobedience,
> To break away, to turn from your embrace,
> And choose the shackles of sin's slavery, the death of innocence?[2]

In keeping with the Trinitarian ordering of this book, I wish to
propose grace as the particular and distinguishing mark of God the
Father or Creator and first person in the Christian Trinity. I am well
aware that the New Testament quite often attributes grace specifically
to Jesus Christ, the second person of the Trinity, as in 2 Corinthians

13.14 quoted above, and in the very last words of the Bible: 'the grace of our Lord Jesus Christ be with all the saints' (Revelation 22. 21). On other occasions, grace is portrayed as an attribute shared by Father and Son, as in Paul's greeting to the various Christian communities to which he writes, repeated ten times in his letters: 'Grace and peace to you, from God our Father and the Lord Jesus Christ.' This greeting presents grace as one of the principal themes in God's communication with humanity. Grace is, indeed, central to God's self-communication, and in Christian understanding this means that it is particularly associated with the communication and expression of God in the person of his Son. In Christian tradition, grace is particularly associated with God becoming flesh in Jesus Christ. In the majestic words from the prologue of St John's Gospel: 'The Word became flesh and dwelt among us full of grace and truth' (John 1.14). What is striking here is the way in which grace is seen as the first characteristic of the Word and therefore the most fundamental expression of the Incarnation. The prologue continues: 'From his fullness we have all received grace heaped upon grace' – in the Greek και καριν αντι καριτος (John 1.16). This wonderful language of extravagant and overflowing love of course applies to the person of Jesus Christ as much as to God the Father, but it is specifically directed at Christ's role as the incarnation of God. Grace infuses and suffuses the whole Triune Godhead, but it is perhaps the special and outstanding property of that being or person within it particularly associated with the work of creation and bringing to be.

In those monotheistic faiths which do not have a Trinitarian perspective, grace is seen as a central characteristic of the divine creator. Jews have a strong sense of the graciousness of God which goes back to the oft-repeated mantra in the Psalms, 'Thou, O Lord, art a God merciful and gracious, slow to anger and abounding in steadfast love and faithfulness.' In the Hebrew Bible, three different words express the idea of divine grace – *hesed*, which describes God's faithful maintenance of the covenant relationship with his people; *hanan*, which means the gratuitous gift of affection; and *raham*, a broad term from the root *rahm* which embraces the ideas of mercy, compassion and forgiveness. These attributes of steadfast love, faithfulness, mercy and compassion are seen as standing alongside other divine characteristics such as righteousness and judgement. The tension between them is acknowledged and the narrative of the Hebrew Bible is interpreted in Jewish tradition as indicating a clear shift on the part of God from an emphasis on judgement to a preference for mercy. In the words of Rashi, an influential eleventh-century commentator: 'in the beginning, God sought to create the world through the attribute of justice, but He saw that it could not stand. What then did He do? He took justice and joined to it the attribute of mercy.'[3] This divine change of heart in the direction of grace and mercy is evident in the story told in the early chapters of Genesis. Faced with human disobedience, God initially regrets creating men and women and brings a flood which only Noah and his family survive. Emerging from the ark, Noah brings an offering to God, who is moved with compassion and declares, 'Never again will I curse the ground because of man.' This change of heart is expressed in a covenant made not just with Noah but with all living creatures. As Jonathan Sacks observes:

> This is forgiveness as an act of grace, a unilateral decision on the part of God. There has been no apology, no remorse, no act of restitution . . . The rainbow covenant is a declaration, as it were, of pre-emptive forgiveness. God binds himself in advance to temper justice with mercy. He accepts that he cannot expect perfection from mankind.[4]

Much recent Christian Old Testament scholarship accepts this Jewish exegesis of the Hebrew Bible and sees divine grace in terms of a change of mind, or at least a progressive revelation, on the part of God from narrow justice and retribution towards mercy and forgiveness. This shift of emphasis is clearly seen in the book of Exodus where God's successive appearances to Moses show a progressive move away from anger and punishment towards steadfast love and mercy. Perhaps more than any other book in the Bible, Exodus reflects what one of its most recent commentators, Dennis Olson, calls 'the compelling dialectical tensions: divine judgement versus divine mercy, God's sovereignty versus God's suffering and compassion, God's nearness and God's otherness'.[5] Both sides to the divine character are very clearly present in Moses' first encounter with God in the form of the burning bush (Exodus 3.1—4.31). In Olson's words, 'The burning bush expresses both God's merciful accommodation, coming down from the mountain of God to meet Moses, and God's awesome holiness, the unquenchable fire being both dangerous and attractive at the same time.'[6] In his next significant revelation to Moses, God declares himself first and foremost as jealous and punishing and only secondarily as showing steadfast love (Exodus 20.5–6). In the final and most significant theophany, however, the Lord is revealed as 'a God merciful and gracious, slow to anger, and abounding in steadfast love and faithfulness, keeping steadfast love for thousands, forgiving inquity and transgression and sin' (Exodus 34.6–7). The conditionality expressed in the earlier revelation, where God indicates love only 'to those who love me and keep my commandments' is dropped. Disobedience will continue to generate consequences, but divine judgement now occupies a secondary role to divine mercy.

These progressively more liberal statements about God's basic character in the book of Exodus are significant in at least two respects. They suggest a progressive, ongoing revelation by and of God through scripture which is perhaps consonant with liberal notions of continuing post-scriptural revelation discussed later in this book (see pages 107–8). They also give an impression of God as being sensitive to changing situations and moved to compassion by human weakness and folly rather than as a static, stern, unmoveable judge. There are, of course, other examples in the Old Testament where God apparently undergoes a change of mind, and where an initial impulse to punish and exact vengeance gives way to a disposition to forgive and show mercy, notably over the fate of Nineveh in the book of Jonah.

In Islam there is if anything an even clearer emphasis on God's mercy predominating over God's wrath. The two names for Allah which occur at the beginning of nearly every *sura* or chapter of the Koran, *al-Rahman* and *al-Rahim*, both derive from the Arabic root *rahm* with its connotations of the womb. They are usually translated as 'the compassionate' and 'the merciful'. For Muslims, mercy is the pre-eminent characteristic of God. The word occurs 200 times in the Koran quite apart from its appearance at the start of chapters. Sura 40 is entitled 'The Forgiving One' and Sura 55 'The Merciful'. God's mercy has a universal aspect – 'Lord, you embrace all things with your mercy' (Sura 40.7) – and governs the ordering of the world – 'he who is ever merciful orders, regulates, rules and bestows in pursuance of mercy'. What is experienced on earth is just a tiny portion of the sum total of God's mercy which has been divided into 100 portions, with just one portion being sent down to earth and divided among every loving family and every tender relationship throughout the human and animal kingdoms. The remaining 99 portions remain to be showered on faithful believers in the afterlife. As in Judaism and Christianity, there is an acknowledgement of the tension between God's mercy and righteous indignation. Islam is clear about the priority of mercy. Among the key statements in the *Hadith*, the collection of sayings of the prophet Muhammad which supplement the Koran, is 'When God created the creation, He wrote beneath His throne: "My mercy overcomes my wrath".' It has to be said that divine wrath remains a very prominent theme in the Koran, especially as it is directed to non-believers. The accent, however, is always on mercy. Islam balances the oneness and greatness of God with a magnanimity and generosity which is the foundation for human freedom and responsible creaturehood. It is perhaps worth noting here that in Islam there is no sense of original sin being transmitted like a hereditary disease from generation to generation and of the tiny baby being somehow a sinner. Every human being is seen as being born innocent but with free will and a capacity to choose either good or wrong.

The Koran's emphasis on mercy as the great attribute of God is given expression in some beautifully poetic language: 'He sends forth the winds as harbingers of his mercy, and when they have gathered up a heavy cloud, We drive it on to some dead land and let the water fall upon it, bringing forth all manner of fruit' (Surah 7.55). This image of mercy being gathered up in a cloud so that it may fall on some particularly barren land is remarkably similar to that used by Shakespeare in the famous lines given to Portia in *The Merchant of Venice* just before she reflects that 'it is an attribute to God himself':

> The quality of mercy is not strain'd;
> It droppeth as the gentle rain from heaven
> Upon the place beneath: it is twice bless'd;
> It blesseth him that gives and him that takes.
>
> (Act IV, Scene 1)

In Indian religions the idea of divine grace is central to the *Saiva Siddh nta* tradition which emphasizes the soul's progress from bondage to liberation. It is conceived in terms of two concepts – *akti*, translated as both grace and power, which starts the whole process of evolution and goes on to accomplish the flowering of creation and lead the evolving soul to liberation, and *Arul*, the love that is neither merited not deserved and from which God gains no benefit. It is this grace that destroys a person's last karma and liberates the individual from the cycle of birth and death. In the *Srivaisnava* tradition there is a similar understanding of divine grace, here called *krpa*, which ends a human's karma and brings liberation from the cycle of birth and death. It involves no human effort and entails the belief that the Lord enjoys and accepts the faults of his devotees. Both traditions see grace as an entirely unmerited free gift from God with an essentially liberating function.[7]

In Christianity, too, there is an emphasis on the unmerited forgiveness at the heart of God's grace and its almost recklessly extravagant generosity. These aspects are perhaps best illustrated in the parable of the prodigal son where the father runs out to meet and embrace his less than wholly repentant ne'er-do-well son who has squandered his inheritance. It is hard to over-emphasize the scandalous nature of this gesture in first-century Palestinian society. A wealthy and respectable householder would never have thought of running even if his robes had allowed him to do so. Here is a father who quite literally loses his dignity in reaching out to his errant son and showing him unconditional forgiveness and acceptance. This is not cheap grace but a love that bears all things, hopes all things and endures all things.

There is a similar picture of God's grace at work in the parable of the lost sheep and the image of the shepherd's special concern for the one who has gone astray. Henry Baker's allusion to this parable in his rather free paraphrase of the 23rd Psalm, 'The King of Love My Shepherd Is', points up the importance of the themes of hospitality and homecoming in the workings of divine grace:

> Perverse and foolish oft I strayed,
> And yet in love he sought me,
> And on his shoulders gently laid
> And home rejoicing brought me.

The Gospels portray Jesus embodying, teaching and living out God's grace and forgiveness. In marked contrast to the prevailing customs and practices of his time, place and people, he practises the radical inclusivity of the open table, eating with tax collectors, sinners and prostitutes, refusing to condemn the woman taken in adultery, reaching out to Zacchaeus before he has shown any signs of repentance, and wilfully ignoring rules and taboos about cleanliness and purity in his dealings with Jairus' daughter and the woman suffering from continuous haemorrhages. His parables, like his actions, speak of gratuituous, unearned and unconditional acceptance. Those who encountered Jesus experienced that sense of being 'sought in love' that Baker's hymn so beautifully invokes. It is an experience shared by many who have felt the restorative and liberating power of divine grace. Some of the most moving testimonies to its beneficial effects are from those who have themselves been in the position of the prodigal son, the haemorrhaging woman, or the woman caught in adultery, again and again, wondering how they can possibly break out of the cycle of despair and start afresh. For them, grace is about having the slate wiped clean and being given yet another chance, as for this contributor to the magazine sold by the homeless, *The Big Issue*:

> How often he has picked me up,
> How often dried my tears,
> Held me close, calmed and soothed
> And loved away my fears.
>
> How often has he sent me back
> To take up the cross again
> And ringing in my ears the words,
> Neither do I condemn.
>
> How often grace like snow has fallen.
> Grace on grace, grace on grace,
> Until defiance, deceit and selfish lies
> Have vanished before his face.[8]

For the author of that poem, as for the prodigal son and the woman caught in adultery, grace is experienced as forgiveness, acceptance and the chance to escape from a broken, dysfunctional life that has become a living hell. It is through the power of grace that God brings liberation from the bondage, the brokenness, the alienation and the frustration that characterize so many human lives. Grace in these situations brings trust, wholeness, reconciliation, and often, too, unmerited forgiveness. But God's grace is not just limited to such situations of wrong-doing or disaster that require an emergency rescue package. It is proactive as well as reactive, being the very essence of God and pointing to the foundational goodness and generosity at the heart of the Creator as much as to a propensity to pull people out of trouble and rescue them from sin and despair.

It is here that we come to a difference in emphasis between liberal and evangelical understandings of grace. For evangelicals just as much as for liberals, grace is a central theological theme. But whereas liberals tend to emphasize the primary, foundational, prevenient nature of God's grace and to see it in terms of a disposition to bless, evangelicals, while acknowledging what they call 'common grace', tend to lay more stress on the specifically salvific and redeeming aspects of what they refer to as 'saving grace'. P. T. Forsyth demonstrates this evangelical emphasis in his comment that 'the trust of Grace is greater than the obedience that never strayed from Love and knows no repentance. It is a greater God that redeems than just blesses.'[9] Most liberals would agree with this assessment which takes us back to the link between grace and freedom highlighted in Alan Gaunt's hymn quoted above. They would, however, want to suggest that the God who blesses is as great as the God who redeems and that both aspects of the divine being are to be equally emphasized and valued. In the conservative evangelical tradition, God's grace has been primarily conceived of and valued in terms of its salvific properties – it is first and foremost about salvation from sin. This connection is very clearly spelled out in the title of John Bunyan's classic *Grace Abounding to the Chief of Sinners* and in the opening line of John Newton's great hymn 'Amazing grace, how sweet the sound that saved a wretch like me'. For liberals, grace abounds not just for sinners and in order to deal with sin. It does undoubtedly have a salvific function. Contrary to Niebuhr's caricature, liberals do not

believe that a God without wrath brings men without sin into a
kingdom without judgement. They acknowledge the deep flaws and
failings that exist both among individuals and in society. They also
acknowledge God's holiness and the offence that human behaviour
must so often provoke. We all fall short and we all stray, and it is God's
mercy and forgiveness that lift us up and bring us home, just as in the
parables of the prodigal son and the lost sheep. However, for the liberal
believer, to focus simply and exclusively on the relationship between
grace and sin is to belittle God and narrow the scope and purpose of
God's dealings with humanity. God's grace is not just encountered
through the experience of being saved; it has many other dimensions.
Julian of Norwich experienced it in terms of an overwhelming sense
that 'everything has its being through the love of God' and that 'all
shall be well, and all shall be well, and all manner of things shall be
well':

> I saw without a doubt that before he created us, God loved us, and
> his love remains constant. All his works have been done in this
> love, and it is this love that gives us everlasting life. Our beginning
> was in our making, but the love which made us has no beginning:
> it is in this love that we have our beginning, and which we shall see
> in God without end.[10]

An analysis of Newton's 'Amazing Grace' shows more clearly the
different points of emphasis between evangelicals and liberals on the
subject of grace. It is rightly an iconic and hugely popular hymn that
has helped many people in times of despair and darkness. Its third and
fourth verses wonderfully articulate the message of the parables of the
prodigal son and the lost sheep that 'grace will lead me home' and
express the themes of hope and promise with which this book ends.
Its first two verses, however, contain three phrases which, rightly or
wrongly, stick in the liberal throat and underline significant differences
of emphasis between evangelical and liberal understandings of grace.
The first is the line 'that saved a wretch like me'. It epitomizes a classic
evangelical emphasis on the radical wretchedness of humanity, applied
especially to oneself, also expressed in the phrase 'Foul, I to the
fountain fly' in the hymn 'Rock of Ages' and in Isaac Watts' self-

description in his hymn 'Alas! and did my Saviour bleed' as 'such a worm as I'. Liberals would want to ask how helpful and healthy it is to describe people, not least oneself, in these terms and to suggest that it can be psychologically and spiritually very damaging.

Evangelical friends who have read this book in manuscript tell me that, like all liberals, I have not made enough of the sinfulness and wretchedness of the human condition and not looked enough into the dark corners of my own life to find and identify 'the rats in the cellar' as one of them put it. Maybe a certain naive optimism about the human condition (and one's own state in particular) and a tendency to emphasize original goodness over original sin is the great liberal heresy. I cannot, however, find a call to gloomy and morbid introspection and radical self-denigration at the heart of Jesus' gospel and his dealings with people. Rather his mission and aim seem directed at building up and affirming human beings, remembering that they are created in the image of God, however far they are from what they might be. It is perhaps relevant to remember the circumstances of Newton's own early life and the crisis which led him to write this hymn. While none of us are without sin, not all have pursued lives of such extremes and gone through such dramatic conversion experiences. I find myself wondering again whether at least part of the difference of view between evangelicals and liberals on this as on other points is explicable in terms of very different life experiences and psychological make-ups (see pages 158–9). I trust that it is not liberal self-satisfaction or naivety that makes me uneasy about the grovelling self-condemnatory language of certain classic evangelical hymnwriters but rather a sense that it limits God's grace by linking it narrowly and almost exclusively to human sin and does not do full justice to the gracious goodness of God in creation, and the fact that we are all created in God's image, however far we have fallen short.

The second phrase in Newton's hymn that is calculated to make liberals uneasy comes in the opening line of the second verse, ''Twas grace that taught my heart to fear'. It is admittedly immediately balanced by the statement in the next line 'and grace my fears relieved' but it still gives the message that grace is linked to fear and, indeed, that it should somehow inspire and lead to fear. This seems to me the antithesis of the Christian gospel as I understand and follow it. The grace of the prodigal's father does not teach his son to fear, any more than does the grace shown by Jesus to the woman taken in adultery. Rather, it surrounds them with acceptance, love and affirmation. It is certainly true that God should inspire an attitude of awe and reverence on the part of us, God's creatures. The text, 'the fear of the Lord is the beginning of wisdom' (Psalm 111.10) is one with which liberals in particular need to wrestle and engage, and I force myself to meditate and preach on it at regular intervals. However, the exercise of fear and the implanting of fear in those with whom God has dealings is surely not what grace is about. God does not rule us through fear but rather relates to us in love.

> God is love, and he who abides in love abides in God, and God in him. In this is love perfected in us, that we may have confidence in the day of judgment, because as he is so are we in this world. There is no fear in love, but perfect love casts out fear. For fear has to do with punishment, and he who fears is not perfected in love. (1 John 4.16–18)

This is an extraordinarily significant statement. It suggests that all who abide in love abide in God, regardless of whether they are consciously Christians or even theists. It has considerable implications for a Christian understanding of religious pluralism and approach to other faiths. It also makes crystal clear that there is no room or place for fear or punishment in the exercise of God's grace. Indeed, far from teaching our hearts to fear, God's loving grace casts out fear and gives us confidence for the day of judgement. Grace dispels fear – its whole function and purpose is to turn our hearts from loathing, including self-loathing, to love.

The third phrase in Newton's hymn which conveys an essentially evangelical rather than liberal perspective is 'how precious did that grace appear the hour I first believed'. This ties the appreciation of grace, if not its actual efficacy, to the moment of belief, the sudden and decisive conversion experience so important in evangelical theology. It strongly suggests that only the believer can really and truly experience grace, which comes almost as an adjunct of conversion. For liberals, and indeed within orthodox Christian tradition, grace is prevenient and unconditional. It reaches out and flows over us before we are ever aware of it or invoke it ourselves. God loves us before we make any move towards God, just as the prodigal's father rushed out to meet and embrace his wayward son before he had any idea of his state of mind. It is in response to God's grace and as those embraced and touched by it that we approach God. In the words of 1 John 4.19: 'We love because he first loved us.' The difference between liberals' and evangelicals' understanding on this point is well illustrated in their respective attitudes to infant baptism. Liberals are strongly in favour of baptizing babies and infants because this practice perfectly demonstrates the doctrine of prevenient grace. It does not matter that the one being baptized cannot understand what is happening. In the sacrament, God's overflowing prevenient grace is poured out in a demonstrable sign that God loves us before we love God. Most evangelicals, by contrast, believe that only believers should be baptized. As in Newton's hymn, grace is linked to 'the hour I first believed'. For liberals, this approach involves a limitation of God's grace. It becomes conditional, and the initiative and emphasis shifts from God to the individual – I rather than God become the focus with the insistence that grace is imputed when an individual has a definite and particular conversion experience. The danger here is that grace becomes a personal possession – something that I receive all to myself when I make my conversion. This is the antithesis of grace. As Leonard Kotzbauer has written: 'Grace benefits everyone. Grace can never be a thing possessed because it is a light unceasingly emanating from and returning to God.'[11]

Powerful and iconic though it undoubtedly is, John Newton's 'Amazing Grace' exemplifies a theology of grace which is, for liberals, flawed and incomplete. It conceives of grace simply in terms of salvation from sin, encourages a negative, grovelling view of humanity and posits a somewhat cold and calculating God who instils fear and almost seems to offer grace as a *quid pro quo* for belief. Liberals would want to express the relationship between God and humanity in a very different way, with grace not being restricted to saving individuals from sin but conceived of as a quality of overflowing generosity, sensitivity and openness enabling each life to be lived to the full. A good contemporary example is Jim Cotter's refrain for his re-working of Psalm 144:

> O Lover, divine and human,
> intimate, insistent and tender,
> courteous in paying attention,
> passionate in wholehearted embrace,
> bring us alive and alight,
> each a singular creation.[12]

The different understandings of grace between liberals and conservative evangelicals come to a head in the interpretation of God's work in
and through Christ, and specifically through the death of Jesus, in what
is known in theological parlance as the atonement. It is important to
acknowledge that there is no single evangelical view on the atonement,
any more than there is a single liberal view. Most evangelicals, however,
believe in what is called substitutionary atonement – that Jesus died
intentionally and willingly on the cross as a propitiation, or substitute,
for sinners – with the more conservative believing in penal substitution,
Jesus' death being a punishment in the place of sinners to satisfy the
demands of a righteous and angry God for justice. The theory of penal
substitution is perhaps most clearly stated by Calvin:

> God was the enemy of men until they were restored to favour by
> the death of Christ. They were cursed until their iniquity was
> expiated by the sacrifice of Christ.
>
> Christ interposed, took the punishment upon himself and bore
> what by the just judgement of God was impending over sinners;
> with his own blood satisfied and duly propitiated, God the Father,
> by this intercession appeased his anger.[13]

For liberals, this reading of the central and terrible drama of the cross
that stands at the heart of Christianity is abhorrent. It suggests a
brutal and sadistic deity who can only be propitiated by the spilling of
blood and who derives satisfaction from the agonizing death of his
own Son. Liberals do not seek to deny the reality nor the scandal of
the crucifixion but they refuse to see it as a sin offering in which Jesus
is killed as a substitute for sinful humanity in order to placate and
appease his angry, vengeful, judging Father. Rather, they see the cross
as an anguished expression of the costly self-giving and self-sacrifice

that lies at the very heart of the divine being and is central to God's grace.

Liberal Christian voices down the ages, from Origen and Abelard to William Channing and Horace Bushnell, have vigorously opposed the doctrine of penal substitution. Sadly, on the back of the Fundamentals of 1910–15, the doctrine has boomed over the last hundred years, although it is increasingly being called into question from within the evangelical world. It received a recent popular endorsement in Mel Gibson's film *The Passion of the Christ*. The best liberal critique of this film that I know of has come from Richard Rohr, a Franciscan friar and founder for the Center for Contemplation and Action in New Mexico, who invokes the arguments of another of the great medieval opponents of substitutionary atonement theory, John Duns Scotus:

> Jesus did not have to die to make God love us, he was paying no debt, he was changing no Divine mind. Jesus was only given to change our minds about the nature of God! Imagine what we are saying about the Father if he needed blood from his son to decide to love us! It is an incoherent world with no organic union between Creator and creature. No wonder so few Christians have gone on to the mystical path of love, since God is basically untrustworthy and more than a little dangerous.
>
> For Duns Scotus, Jesus was the 'image of the invisible God' who revealed to us God's eternal suffering love for humanity in an iconic form that we could not forget. He was not 'necessary' but a pure gift. The suffering was simply to open our hearts, not to open God's which was always open. Unfortunately, the movie is entirely based on the old atonement theory that suffering was needed, the more suffering the better and the most suffering the best of all. Unfortunately, this has been the mainline tradition, and has been made into dogma by evangelical Christians. It creates a mercantile Christianity with God as the major debt collector, when what Jesus came to offer was a mystical Christianity with God as the 'bride-groom'.[14]

Liberals differ as to how they understand the atonement and Jesus' death. Some are uneasy about invoking the concept of sacrifice at all, following Jesus' approving quotation of the prophet Hosea: 'I desire mercy and not sacrifice' (Matthew 9.13). I myself have argued at some length that Christians should not abandon what is undoubtedly an impenetrable and off-putting concept but rather rethink their attitude towards the whole subject of sacrifice, seeing it not primarily as something that is done to God, either by humans or by Christ on our behalf, but rather as the principle which is eternally at the very heart and centre of the life of the Holy Trinity and the divine purpose and plan for creation.[15] In this understanding, the cross is indeed a sacrifice but one that reveals the self-sacrificial nature of God and which is directed as much to suffering as to sinful humanity. It is indeed the supreme expression of that gratuitous, overflowing, unmerited grace that flows from the heart of the Godhead. Other liberals will have different emphases and perspectives, but what all share is a rejection of the notion of grace as an emergency rescue package brought in as a remedy for sin and involving the paying of a price, the satisfaction of a debt or the exaction of a punishment. Some, though by no means all, evangelicals further limit the scope of God's grace by seeing it as essentially conditional, either on the act of conversion and believing or, in the gloomier aspects of Calvinism, on election and predestination. Liberals want rather to affirm the wide, spacious, unlimited and unconditional nature of God's grace and mercy.

Unfortunately some of the best-loved hymns which are the chief means by which we learn and reinforce our theology propagate the idea of substitutionary atonement and situate God's grace in the context of the court room or the counting house. However, there are other classic hymns that speak of God's grace not in forensic and mercantile language but in terms of a fundamental prevenient disposition to love. Samuel Crossman's 'My Song is Love Unknown' comes close to expounding an Abelardian exemplary theory of atonement in its statement that Christ's death represents 'love to the loveless shown that they might lovely be'. Henry Lyte's 'Praise My Soul the King of Heaven' praises God 'for his grace and favour . . . slow to chide and swift to bless'.

There is one quite outstanding hymnological encapsulation of God's grace in all its overflowing generosity and openness. It is the work of Frederick William Faber (1814–63), who is not normally thought of as a liberal and who moved from extreme evangelicalism to high Anglicanism under the influence of the Oxford Movement and thence to Roman Catholicism. Whatever his churchmanship, however, these verses by Faber constitute one of the finest expressions of the liberal theology of grace.

> There's a wideness in God's mercy,
> Like the wideness of the sea;
> There's a kindness in his justice
> Which is more than liberty.
>
> There is no place where earth's sorrows
> Are more felt than up in heaven:
> There is no place where earth's failings
> Have such kindly judgement given.
>
> There is grace enough for thousands
> Of new worlds as great as this:
> There is room for fresh creations
> In that upper home of bliss.
>
> For the love of God is broader
> Than the measures of man's mind;
> And the heart of the Eternal
> Is most wonderfully kind.
>
> But we make his love too narrow
> By false limits of our own;
> And we magnify his strictness
> With a zeal he will not own.
>
> If our love were but more simple,
> We should take him at his word;
> And our lives would be all sunshine,
> In the sweetness of our Lord.

Maybe it is not so surprising that these verses were written by an ardent Roman Catholic – Faber penned them shortly after he set up the Brompton Oratory in London of which he remained Superior for the rest of his life. The Roman Catholic view of grace as a habit or quality infused into humans by God tends to be more inclusive, dynamic and positive than the classic Protestant teaching that it involves imputed righteousness whereby it is Christ's deeds on our behalf through which humans are accounted righteous and saved. The Reformation somewhat skewed and distorted the essentially positive understanding of grace widely held in the Middle Ages and beautifully expressed by Thomas Aquinas: 'As the sun pours light into the air, so God pours grace into the soul.' As Tina Beattie, Professor of Catholic Studies at Roehampton University, has recently observed, 'The medieval view of the innate goodness of a Creation that shivered and shimmered with divine grace yielded to the more pessimistic theology of the reformers, for whom original sin had catastrophically severed the human mind from its capacity to recognize God in nature.'[16]

It is perhaps no coincidence that one of the best-worked-out modern theologies of grace, particularly appealing to liberals, should come from Karl Rahner, arguably the leading Roman Catholic theologian of the twentieth century. For him, grace is not some ethereal substance or created gift but God's self-communication and specifically God's giving of himself to the depths of every individual human consciousness. The world was created for the sake of God's gracious self-communication – that is its reason for being. Uncreated grace has existed from all time and is constantly and unconditionally available. All human beings are constantly experiencing God as graciously offering himself. One does not have to recognize this explicitly as an experience of grace in order to accept or reject it – rather, we accept or reject it insofar as at some level we fundamentally accept or reject ourselves. In Rahner's understanding, all grace is the grace of Christ, and it therefore becomes possible to suggest that those of any religious persuasion whatsoever may without realizing it accept and experience the grace of Christ. They will not necessarily concur in this reading of their situation, but persuading them to regard themselves as Christian is not part of his agenda. They are, in his phrase, anonymous Christians.[17]

This is a classic expression of what is known as the inclusivist position in terms of different Christian responses to those of other faiths. For some engaged in inter-faith dialogue today, the idea of 'anonymous Christianity' is too imperialistic and patronizing. They prefer a pluralistic position where all faiths are seen as equally valid and there is no attempt to bring them together under the broad embrace of Christ. Rahner's approach does, however, have the undoubted merit of emphasizing the breadth and the universal reach of the grace that he sees as essentially synonymous with God as revealed in Christ.

Grace is not just the prime attribute of God, if not indeed God's very self and being. It is also a key human attribute, by virtue both of humanity's creation in the image of God and of the constant infusion of grace into God's creatures. In a very real sense, grace begets grace. It is, of course, not an exclusively or peculiarly liberal value – there are graceless liberals around, just as there are grace-filled conservatives – but when displayed by humans it does express and embody that broad, open-minded and open-hearted generosity that the Authorized Version of the Bible describes with the word 'liberal'. Liberal theology is nothing if it is not gracious. Indeed, I would go so far as to say that liberals are called to be gracious – by this I have in mind not just the general Christian calling to be vulnerable, to turn the other cheek and walk the extra mile, but a more specific and more demanding vocation to gentility, generosity, openness and not judging people. It is the very opposite of the triumphalism, strident certainty, tendency to judge and insensitivity that characterize fundamentalists of every hue. Fundamentalists cannot comprehend the graciousness of liberalism which they simultaneously misunderstand and pooh-pooh as a wishy-washy lack of conviction over-ready to see the other side and the opposite point of view. In a world of increasing fundamentalism and fear, we need more than ever the values and the voice of grace-filled and gracious liberalism.

What are these values? They can, I think, be grouped into three principal heads: a disposition to forgive; a concern for the pastoral dimension in any given situation or dispute; and an outlook of generosity and blessing. These seem to me to be the particular marks of a liberal theology of grace, and all three are sorely needed today both in the spheres of politics and economics and within the Christian Church and other faith communities.

Forgiveness, as we have seen, is a key aspect of God's grace as it is understood in all major religious traditions. It is also a quality that humans are called on to practise, notably in the teaching of the three great Abrahamic faiths. This is clearly demonstrated in the centrality of the story of Joseph forgiving his brothers in Judaism, Christianity and Islam. Jonathan Sacks describes the Joseph story, which is found in Genesis 50, verses 15 to 21 and in Sura 12 of the Koran as 'the Bible's most extended essay on the concept of forgiveness'.[18] After their father's death, Joseph's brothers are convinced that he is going to hate them because of the way they treated him out of their jealousy that he was their father's favourite. They had cast him into a pit and sold him into slavery. Now that the tables are turned, and they find themselves destitute and at his mercy while he is rich and powerful, the trusted adviser and friend of the ruler of Egypt, they expect him to repay them in kind for the evil they have done him. They anticipate receiving an eye for an eye and a tooth for a tooth – that is their kind of justice. Joseph, however, reacts very differently. He tells them to get up off their knees and speaks kindly to them. His outlook, directly informed by his belief in and dependence on God, is one of mercy and forgiveness, not of vengeance.

An even more powerful and explicit injunction to forgive is contained in the New Testament parable of the king and his servants. Moved to pity, the king cancels the debt of a servant who owes him 10,000 talents. However, that servant himself has the 'eye for an eye and tooth for a tooth' mentality of Joseph's brothers. Although forgiven his own huge debt, he is quite unwilling to forgive the relatively trivial debt of just 100 *denarii* which he is owed by a fellow-servant. The unforgiving servant is summoned by the king and sent to gaol until he has paid his debt. Jesus ends the story by telling his disciples: 'So also my heavenly Father will do to every one of you, if you do not forgive your brother from your heart' (Matthew 18.35). The Koran teaches a similar message: 'Show mercy to others: God will show mercy to you . . . To forgive is a duty incumbent on all . . . He that forgives and shows reconcilement shall be rewarded by Allah' (Suras 42.9, 43).

The link made here between divine and human mercy is crucial. In Jewish, Christian and Islamic understanding, the one follows the other.

God in his infinite mercy forgives us all our failings, shortcomings and sins when we turn to God in repentance. As forgiven creatures, we should in turn show compassion and forgiveness towards those who have offended and slighted us. Jesus says (Luke 6.36): 'Be compassionate as your Father is compassionate.' The linking of fatherhood, or parenthood, with compassion here is highly significant. Pointing out that the Hebrew and Arabic words for forgiveness both come from the root *rahm*, meaning womb, Jonathan Sacks observes: 'A judge, charged with administering the law cannot forgive, but a parent can. The concept of forgiveness comes into existence when God is envisaged as both judge and parent; when law and love, justice and mercy, join hands. God forgives, and in so doing, teaches us to forgive.'[19]

We are brought back to the prevenience of God's grace and its power to beget grace in us. God's forgiveness inspires our forgiveness. Just as we love God because God first loved us, so we forgive others because God forgives us. God's freely given, overflowing grace cascades downwards. It is as God's forgiven and loved creatures that we can in turn forgive. We pray to God in the Lord's Prayer, 'forgive us our sins as we forgive those who sin against us', but this is really the wrong way round. What we should be praying is, 'May we forgive those who sin against us as you have forgiven us our sins.' There is a wonderful reciprocity and mutual interchange here, although it does not make the practice of forgiveness an easy option. Rather, it is a matter of costly and constant forbearance and generosity of spirit: 'When your brother wrongs you seven times a day and seven times comes back to you and says "I am sorry" you must forgive him' (Luke 17.4). Jesus himself utters his ultimate plea for errant humanity from the cross: 'Father, forgive them. They don't know what they are doing' (Luke 23.34). This expression of forgiveness is not just directed to the Father by his Son – it is within the mystery and the agony of the Trinity in a very real sense the word of the crucified God.

It is not just God's forgiveness that begets and inspires human forgiveness. Something similar happens when one human forgives another. This is graphically illustrated in Victor Hugo's great novel, *Les Misérables*, and in the hugely popular musical based on it. The central character, Jean Valjean, is redeemed and transformed by the act of forgiveness shown towards him by the saintly Bishop of Digne after he has stolen his silverware. This one act of grace changes Valjean from a self-pitying misanthropist to a model of sacrificial love and service. He is contrasted with Javert, the police inspector who is determined to hunt him down and who adheres to the narrow, vengeful 'eye for an eye and tooth for a tooth' mentality of Joseph's brothers and the servant in Jesus' parable. When Valjean has the chance of getting even with his pursuer on the revolutionaries' barricades in Paris but instead spares his life, Javert cannot cope with this act of forgiveness and ends up committing suicide. The story underlines the transformative nature of forgiveness if the one being forgiven is prepared to change. The antithesis of forgiveness is the narrow judgemental code followed by Joseph's brothers and Javert which naturally judges and condemns others and expects judgement and condemnation in return. It is the fundamentalists' creed and it is a temptingly easy mindset for all of us to fall into when we are confronted by those whom we regard as our enemies or even those who are different from us in their beliefs and practices.

Forgiveness is a supremely liberal virtue. It is liberating both for forgiver and forgiven. It is about being open to the future rather than imprisoned by the past. It is grounded in what Jonathan Sacks in this eloquent meditation calls 'the unpredictability of grace'.

> In a world without forgiveness, evil begets evil, harm generates harm, and there is no way short of exhaustion or forgetfulness of breaking the sequence. Forgiveness breaks the chain. It introduces into the logic of interpersonal encounter the unpredictability of grace. It represents a decision not to do what instinct and passion urge us to do. It answers hate with a refusal to hate, animosity with generosity. Few more daring ideas have ever entered the human situation. Forgiveness means that we are not destined endlessly to replay the grievances of yesterday. It is the ability to live with the past without being held captive by the past. It would not be an exaggeration to say that forgiveness is the most compelling testimony to human freedom. It is about the action that is not reaction. It is the refusal to be defined by circumstance. It represents our ability to change course, reframe the narrative of the past and create an unexpected set of possibilities for the future.[20]

In a world dominated by notions of judgement and retaliation, it is this counter-cultural gospel that has inspired such shining examples of forgiveness in action as the Truth and Reconciliation Commission in South Africa. It is desperately needed in Israel/Palestine and other parts of the world in the grip of suspicion and hatred. This is an area where theological and political liberalism walk hand in hand. Inspiring and spreading forgiveness in these and other situations of conflict is far from easy – it is the very opposite of cheap grace – but it is a task to which theological and political liberals alike are called.[21]

The second value at the heart of a liberal theology of grace that we need to reclaim, not least in the churches, is a concern for the pastoral dimension in any given situation or dispute. Indeed, I would go so far as to argue that pastoral concern should be elevated to the same status as scripture, reason and tradition as one of the key criteria according to which the Church comes to a view on difficult and contentious issues. In some respects, this is perhaps somewhat similar to the so-called 'Wesleyan quadrilateral' proposed by John Wesley when he suggested experience as a fourth source of authority in the Church. Experience of life and deep pastoral concern often go hand in hand and effect personal transformations in the direction of a more open, forgiving, grace-filled outlook. I think of the father who completely changes his perspective on homosexuality when his own son comes out as gay, or the grandmother whose views on abortion are transformed by the experience of seeing the effects on her grand-daughter of an unwanted pregnancy. What is happening in both these cases is the prioritizing of love over the law, the pastoral impulse over the tendency to judge and condemn – in short, the operation and application of grace. The trouble is that many in the churches seem to be moving in the opposite direction, erecting dogma over the pastoral dimension. We need to be reminded of William Sloane Coffin's encapsulation of the liberal position that 'in undogmatic caring is our hope'. As Eugene March says, 'the practice of love, not the defence of doctrine, is the primary challenge for Christians (and adherents of other religious traditions as well) in today's world'.[22]

The priority of the pastoral dimension is particularly important in approaching two of the most sensitive and contentious issues of our time – abortion and assisted dying. In a perfect world full of perfect people, maybe there would be no need or call for pregnancies to be terminated. But in the world as it is, there are many circumstances where abortion is the lesser of two evils and where there is a strong pastoral case for terminating a pregnancy. There is a pastoral imperative to meet people where they are. The alternative to legalized abortion is not no abortions at all but botched, dangerous, self-induced or back-street terminations. A recent report from the Guttmacher Institute estimates that over 70,000 women die every year and many more suffer harm as a result of unsafe abortions in countries with restrictive laws on terminating pregnancies. It was the fact that 40 to 50 women died every year as a result of illegal abortions in Britain in the 1960s, with possibly as many again committing suicide, that persuaded David Steel, then a young Liberal MP, to introduce and steer through Parliament the 1967 Abortion Act which effectively established a woman's right to choose, and legalized abortion in the early weeks of pregnancy. The Act has only undergone one minor modification in more than 40 years, with the upper time limit for abortions being reduced from 28 to 24 weeks, and has been a model for similar legislation in other countries. In Steel's own words: 'We did not create abortion on request, we created a state of law where there is a balance between the right of the foetus to develop to full life and the right of women to have what I would call in the biblical phrase "abundant life".'[23]

The use of biblical language here is deliberate and appropriate. David Steel rightly sees no incompatibility between his own Christian faith and his championship of abortion law reform. He cites the Church of England's 1965 report *Abortion: An Ethical Discussion* as a major influence on his own thinking and the best argued document from a Christian standpoint in favour of having a positive law on abortion. Like others supporting legalized abortion, he has suffered attacks from those claiming to represent the Christian viewpoint. As he says, 'What this really means is the viewpoint of the Roman Catholic Church and some of the evangelicals in the Protestant churches but they attach to themselves the adjective Christian.'[24]

There has, in fact, been a significant hardening of views over abortion, especially in the early weeks of pregnancy, on the part of both the Roman Catholic Church and among Protestant evangelicals. Until at least the latter part of the nineteenth century, much Roman Catholic teaching broadly followed the line taken by many medieval theologians that human life effectively begins with the 'quickening' or movement of the foetus in the womb. It is only comparatively recently that the Roman Catholic Church as a whole has taken the line that life begins at the moment of fertilization. The attitude of evangelical Protestants towards abortion has also hardened over recent decades. The Keele Congress, an important gathering of Anglican evangelicals in 1967, issued a statement declaring that the life of the mother, and her physical and mental health, should have priority over the potential personality of the foetus. A gathering of evangelical Christians in 2009 agreed that there would be uproar if an evangelical congress passed such a statement today with its emphasis on the mother's mental as well as physical health and no suggestion that her life must be at stake for abortion to be theologically permissible. Particularly alarming has been the relentless growth of strident and violent fundamentalist opposition to abortion in the United States, as evidenced by the shooting dead of Dr George Tiller in the foyer of his church in Kansas in June 2009. This dangerous movement is characterized by an apparently total lack of grace, forgiveness and pastoral concern. Of course, the views of those who in all conscience oppose abortion should be respected. No one should be forced to have an abortion and no doctor be forced to perform one – a conscience clause to this effect was inserted into David Steel's Bill during its passage through Parliament. But the decisions of those mothers who do decide to terminate pregnancies, often reached after much agonizing, and the compassionate skill, counselling and care shown by medical staff in abortion clinics, should also be affirmed. It may well be that there are too many abortions. However, the remedy for this is not to make the law on abortions more restrictive but to have more and better sex and relationship education and much better provision of birth control services. It is sadly the case that many of those most opposed to abortion are also vehemently against more sex education and easier access to contraception.

A liberal theology of grace would also surely support both voluntary euthanasia and assisted dying for those in terminal illnesses suffering unbearably and explicitly and repeatedly requesting assistance to die and for those with advanced dementia suffering intolerable distress and an abysmal quality of life but incapable of asking for assistance to die. There has been a notable Christian tradition of support for this humane cause. The founding father of the British Voluntary Euthanasia Society, now Dignity in Dying, was R. W. Inge, Dean of St Paul's Cathedral. Polls consistently suggest that a clear majority of Christians across all denominations would support legislation allowing euthanasia for the terminally ill – the figure is sometimes as high as 80 per cent. Yet when Lord Joffe brought forward a Bill to legalize assisted dying in 2006, it was opposed by the leaders of all the major British churches. Almost alone among religious groups, the Modern Church People's Union offered support from a Christian perspective. It was generally agreed by commentators that Lord Joffe's Bill, which contained stringent safeguards, was defeated in large part thanks to a well-orchestrated campaign by Christian organizations and the unanimous opposition of bishops in the House of Lords. The journalist Simon Jenkins observed: 'In years to come, their attitude will be seen not just illiberal but cruel . . . this hangover of religious primitivism must surely end.'[25]

As over abortion, there seems to have been a general retreat from a liberal, humane, pastorally driven approach on the part of church and religious leaders on this issue. A book published in 2009 by Paul Badham does at least and at last provide an eloquent exposition of the Christian case for assisted dying, although it does not cover those with advanced dementia. Arguing on the basis of Jesus' golden rule to treat others as we would wish to be treated ourselves and from the Christian belief in a future life, Badham suggests that it is quite reasonable for Christians to welcome death as bringing relief from the sufferings of terminal illness and quotes Francis of Assisi's invocation of 'O thou most kind and welcome death'. His advocacy of assisted dying is ultimately founded on a theology of grace and compassion: 'When people's sufferings are so great that they make repeated requests to die, it seems a denial of that loving compassion, which is supposed to be the hallmark of Christianity, to refuse to allow their requests to be granted.'[26]

There are many other areas of life where there is a manifest need for a deeper pastoral emphasis and engagement. So often now face-to-face contact is being replaced by a culture of procedure and ticking boxes. Nurses spend more and more time at work-stations filling in forms and less and less at patients' bedsides. A recent report on Britain's residential children's homes found that an emphasis on procedure and the culture of risk aversion and suspicion produced a lack of affection between staff and children. It is not that many health social work professionals want this hands-off and stand-off approach. It is forced on them by increasingly regulated and formalized systems and structures where the emphasis is on doing things by the book rather than making spontaneous human contact.

This brings us to the third value of grace-filled liberalism, an outlook of generosity and blessing. This is in many ways a very counter-cultural approach to adopt in the twenty-first century when, as Adam Phillips and Barbara Taylor have pointed out, generosity and kindness have become the new taboo areas and forbidden pleasures. Their book, *On Kindness*, charts the way in which the value which in the West at least has derived principally from the Christian virtue of *caritas* is now seen as a sign of weakness and has been replaced by a new dominant consensus of ruthless competitive individualism.

> An image of the self has been created that is utterly lacking in natural generosity. Most people appear to believe that deep down they (and other people) are mad, bad and dangerous to know; that as a species – apparently unlike any other species of animal – we are deeply and fundamentally antagonistic to each other, that our motives are utterly self-seeking.[27]

This bleak secular pessimism about the human condition takes us back to Newton's 'wretch like me' and Watts' 'such a worm as I' but without their evangelical sense of the possibility of redemption and transformation. Liberals must counter it with a theology of generosity that blesses rather than curses, affirms and builds up rather than castigates and pulls down. This does not mean an easy naive optimism that all is for the best in the best of all possible worlds. Rather, it stems from the realization that there is much suffering and misery around but that the way to lift people from it is through generosity and affirmation rather than judgement and criticism. At the end of his moving reflection on the story of the prodigal son, Henri Nouwen charts three stages towards a truly compassionate fatherhood: grief at the sorrow and suffering of the world; constant, unconditional forgiveness; and generosity – 'moving from fear to love'.[28] In similar vein, contemplating the troubled times in which we live, Tina Beattie writes:

> If the Churches have a role to play in all this, then they need to speak the language of grace, hope and promise, not gloom, doom and despair. Yes, we live in worrying times. Yes, greed and exploitation are laying waste our planet and depriving the poor of the means to survive, as well as wreaking psychological and moral havoc in the lives of the rich. But even so, simply piling on more misery, guilt and anxiety is likely to make things worse rather than better. It can only increase the sense of alienation and fear that a culture of excessive individualism and relative affluence leads those who can afford it to surround themselves with the illusory securities of wealth.[29]

Liberal theology recognizes and engages with a world full of pain and sorrow but it also recognizes that grace, like love, is all around, continually overflowing from God and being poured into humanity. This recognition encourages a theology of presence rather than a theology of conversion and mission, an attitude of affirming and upholding people where they are rather than berating them for their failings and sins. In her poem 'Praise We Great Men' dedicated to Benjamin Britten, Edith Sitwell writes:

> Praise we the just –
> Who are not come to judge, but bless
> Immortal things in their poor mortal dress.[30]

This disposition to bless rather than judge is central to liberal theology. It recognizes that *Ubi caritas, ibi Deus est* – where love is, there is God. One of the ways in which we can most clearly display that outlook today is by blessing faithful, loving, same-sex partnerships in church. Sadly, agitation and pressure from conservative evangelicals means that many same-sex couples who have come together out of love and committed themselves to the disciplined structure of a faithful relationship are denied the Church's blessing that they seek.

The liberal ethic of generosity and blessing is needed as much at the international as the individual level. Military leaders are increasingly telling us that militant fundamentalism can only be defeated by winning the battle for hearts and minds and building up an atmosphere of trust rather than through military means alone, still less through the so-called 'war on terror'. How shameful it was to hear the last President of the United States damning the deeply faithful and hospitable inhabitants of a sizeable part of the Middle East as constituting 'an axis of evil', and how heartening to read a Christmas card from the ever-stimulating radical theologian, John Bell, with the following counter-creed:

> We believe in the axis of grace,
> The Commonwealth of the earth,
> The forgiveness of debt,
> The redemption of money,
> The centrality of the meal table,
> The sanctity of the born child,
> The resurrection of hope
> The path to peace
> And life before death.[31]

The 'axis of grace' is actually a rather good encapsulation of the essence of liberal theology. It is an axis that has its origin and centre in God, flows out through the persons of the Trinity and invites all of us to be stewards and agents of that grace through lives in which we exercise generosity, forgiveness, mercy and a ministry of blessing. That is a tall order in a world which is ever more graceless, boorish, selfish and unforgiving and in which liberal grace, far from being cheap, is costly. If we are to reassert and re-establish liberal theology, it must be through our own graciousness in the image of God, following those precepts so beautifully put by Peter in his injunction to the predominantly Gentile Christians scattered through the Roman provinces of Asia Minor:

Above all hold unfailingly your love for one another, since love covers a multitude of sins. Practise hospitality ungrudgingly to one another. As each has received a gift, employ it for one another, as good stewards of God's varied grace. (1 Peter 4.8–10)

Notes

1. A. Hastings (ed.), *The Oxford Companion to Christian Thought* (Oxford: Oxford University Press, 2000), p. 276.
2. 'Eternal God, Supreme in Homeliness'. Text: Alan Gaunt. Copyright © Stainer & Bell, 1998.
3. Sacks 2002, p. 182.
4. Sacks 2002, p. 182.
5. G. O'Day and D. Petersen 2009, p. 27.
6. O'Day and Petersen 2009, p. 29.
7. See M. M. Arulchelvam, 'Our Human Setting According to *Saiva Siddh nta*'' and V. Narayanan, 'Karma, Bhaktiyoga in the Srivaisnava Tradition' in Carter 1992.
8. R. T. Yule, 'Grace On Grace', *The Big Issue in Scotland*, 22–28 February 2001, p. 18.
9. P. T. Forsyth, *The Christian Ethic of War* (London: Longmans Green, 1916), p. 175.
10. Julian of Norwich, *Revelations of Divine Love*, 'Our Lord's Meaning'.
11. Carter 1992, p. 243.
12. J. Cotter, *Out of Silence . . . Into the Silence* (Harlech: Cairns Publications, 2006), p. 427.
13. Calvin, *Institutes of the Christian Religion*, I.xvi.2.
14. Posting by Richard Rohr on John Mark Ministries website, http:/jjm.aaa.net.au.
15. Bradley 1995, *passim*.
16. T. Beattie, 'Thomas for Our Time', *The Tablet*, 6 June 2009, p. 6.
17. For Rahner's understanding of grace see *A Rahner Reader*, ed. G. A. McCool (London: Darton, Longman & Todd, 1975), *Oxford Dictionary of Christian Thought*, p. 593.
18. Sacks 2002, p. 182.
19. Sacks 2002, p. 181.
20. Sacks 2002, pp. 178–9.
21. On the Truth and Reconciliation Commission, see D. Tutu, *No Future Without Forgiveness* (London: Random House, 1999).
22. March 2005, p. x.
23. 'There is No Case for Changing the Abortion Act', *Independent*, 29 April 2008.
24. *Ibid.*
25. *Guardian*, 22 October 2008.
26. P. Badham, *Is there a Christian Case for Assisted Dying?* (London: SPCK, 2009), p. 121.
27. A. Philipps and B. Taylor, *Love Thy Neighbour* (*Guardian Review*, 3 January 2009), p. 2.

28. H. Nouwen, *The Return of the Prodigal Son* (London: Darton, Longman & Todd, 1994), pp. 128–9.
29. T. Beattie, 'Thomas for Our Time', *The Tablet*, 6 June 2009, p. 6.
30. E. Sitwell, *The Outcasts* (London: Macmillan, 1962), p. 19.
31. Text: John L. Bell. Copyright © 2008 WGRG, Iona Community, Glasgow G2 3DH. Reproduced by permission.

4

Order

Several of my liberal friends have implored me to re-name this chapter. For them, order suggests regulation, control and authority, the complete antithesis of the values which stand at the heart of liberalism. It is certainly true that order without grace gives us a cold, heartless God of judgement and vengeance, the God of Javert in *Les Misérables*. That is why I put grace as the first of God's attributes and the primary liberal theological value. With that caveat, however, I stand firm in my belief that order, understood as rhythm, harmony and balance but also as limitation, boundary and self-restraint, is another of the key attributes of God and also one of the central tenets of liberal theology. I find it significant, and not in the least contradictory, that when the British Labour Prime Minister Clement Attlee welcomed delegates to the inaugural General Assembly of the United Nations in 1945 he described the venue for their historic gathering, London's Methodist Central Hall, as 'this ancient home of liberty and order'. Pablo Cassals, the great cellist, similarly paired these two apparently conflicting concepts when he commented that the highest of all artistic ideals was 'freedom with order'. For Cassals, this was the substance of classicism and he quoted approvingly the nineteenth-century violinist, Joseph Joachim's remark that his favourite composers were 'the masters of form who have lost nothing in depth of feeling or free flights of fantasy'.[1]

It is this balance of freedom and order, form and free flights of fantasy, that seems to me to lie at the heart of the being and work of God and also at the heart of the liberal theological outlook. There are several ways of conceiving it. I myself have pointed to the symbolism of the striking decorations found on high-standing Celtic crosses and illuminated manuscripts from the golden age of British and Irish insular Christianity with their interlacing knotwork and ever-twisting spirals encompassed and circumscribed within clearly defined boundaries. They suggest a faith that is in perpetual motion but also has a delicate symmetry and definite pattern, balancing form with free flights of fantasy.[2] As the observations of Cassals and Joachim testify, classical music also displays God's 'good ordering of the world' through its rhythmic organization. In the words of Jeremy Begbie:

> Music shows us in a particularly potent way that dynamic order is possible, that there can be ordered being and becoming, form and vitality, structure and dynamics, flux and articulation. For something to be subject to persistent change need not imply disorder.[3]

There is a long tradition of representing the divine principle of dynamic order through the medium of music. It found particular expression in the medieval idea of *musica mundana*, or music of the spheres. Boethius (c. 480–c. 525), the strongly theistic and Trinitarian Roman philosopher who argued for the existence of God on the basis of the symmetry and balance found in nature, pointed to the order and beauty of the 'vault of heaven' and the harmonious sound made by the rotating crystal spheres to which the heavenly bodies were attached. Richard Rastall has written that in the Middle Ages, 'music was understood as order, and ultimately as the order of the cosmos, whether spiritual or material' and shown how in medieval plays and pageants music was used to represent divine order and especially the order of heaven.[4] The idea of the music of the spheres continued to flourish in the seventeenth and eighteenth centuries. It is well expressed in Joseph Addison's poem, 'The Spacious Firmament on High', which is still sung as a hymn in many Christian denominations. In another poem from the same period, Sir John Davies linked it to the idea of the dance of creation:

> Lo, this is Dancing's true nobility:
> Where all agree, and all in order move;
> Dancing, the art that all arts do approve;
> The fair character of the world's consent,
> The heaven's true figure, and the earth's ornament.[5]

Several contemporary theologians find the combination of form and free flights of fantasy supremely represented in jazz with its improvised variations on a theme. Not being a jazz fan, for me the balance between order and freedom is better expressed in many of the great English hymn tunes of the eighteenth and nineteenth centuries which are broad, expansive, sweeping and open in their melodic and harmonic structure while also clearly conforming to defined laws and principles of composition and harmony. Many of the texts to which they were set and sung, particularly in the nineteenth century, are also markedly broad and liberal in their sentiments. In my experience these tunes suit modern liberal theological texts much better than the late-twentieth-century melodies specifically written to accompany them which seem cramped, dissonant, disordered and less spacious and flowing by comparison.[6]

Order is at the heart of both the being and the work of God, understood as the eternal creative nature that is the cause of the universe, endlessly fashioning form out of chaos, beauty out of brokenness and harmony out of dissonance. It is a fundamental principle in all major faiths. I was struck at a university inter-faith gathering that I convened by the remark of a student who had recently converted to Islam having searched among many religious traditions: 'Through Islam I have been able to put my thoughts in order, to make sense of the world and make the world more beautiful.' He went on to say that Islam had taught him that 'everywhere there is beauty, there is God', so making the key connection between order and grace and between the ordered nature of God's creation and its goodness and beauty.[7] There is a similarly close if at first sight paradoxical connection between order and liberty. Just as a framework of security and stability is needed for the child to grow and achieve true freedom, so order is necessary for creativity, debate and the free exchange of ideas in an atmosphere of tolerance and respect. The words 'Order, order' periodically delivered by the Speaker of the House of Commons are not intended to stifle argument and free speech but rather to keep it in within the civilized, ordered bounds that are necessary, if not essential, for the flourishing of liberal democracy.

The enemy of liberalism is not order but anarchy. This is true in the economic and political sphere as much as in theology. The credit crunch that nearly brought the world to its knees in 2009 was, by common consent, in large part the result of a totally unregulated and uncontrolled banking and credit system underpinned by a *laissez-faire* ideology and a reckless greed and debt culture which was the antithesis of the ordered and structured principles championed by the giants of twentieth-century liberal (and Liberal) economics, J. M. Keynes, William Beveridge and J. K. Galbraith. Just as *laissez-faire* has never been the guiding principle of the British and North American liberal political traditions (see page 96), so anarchy and unbridled freedom are not part of the liberal tradition of theology.

The close relationship between the principles of order and theological liberalism is well expressed in Quakerism, at once the most ordered and the freest of all Christian denominations. One of the first principles that Quakers are enjoined to practise is to 'bring the whole of your life under the ordering of the spirit of Christ'.[8] Quaker worship, based on silence and openness to the Spirit, is, like the Quaker lifestyle, highly disciplined and yet also totally free of dogma and doctrine. Liberal theology also often goes hand in hand with highly structured liturgical worship. In the section on the Church of England in my book about the state of churches in Britain in the early 1990s I wrote:

> Go to evensong at Christ Church Cathedral, Oxford, and you can feast on a banquet of Anglican choral music sung by a choir in candlelight. You can be transported by the timeless and transcendent beauty of seventeenth-century prayers read by canons who in their other incarnation as professors of theology are writing books debunking much of received Christian doctrine. Howells in G and Wiles on *The Myth of God Incarnate* seem to me a fair encapuslation of this apparently incongruous mixture.[9]

It is no accident that liberal preaching and theology are often embedded in highly traditional and liturgical worship. The liturgy provides a structure, a safe and secure home for radical, speculative, imaginative theology. Ordered worship allows space for mystery, contemplation and truths beyond words. This point is well made by Edward Higginbottom, Director of Music at New College, Oxford, in a defence of the Anglican service of Choral Evensong in the face of accusations that it is anachronistic and irrelevant:

The context of Evensong [is] the context of listening, and not the context of commitment or evangelization. This clearly suits many people in today's world, those whose minds are not made up, who wrestle with the complexities of the arguments, but who are nonetheless capable of being drawn into faith through an encounter with the world of the spirit. So I see Evensong as an unusually enabling liturgical environment within the contemporary Church: without confrontation, without the demands of affiliation – rather an engagement with the world of the spirit, and an encouragement to seek truth at an individual's own pace, in his or her own way.[10]

Conservative evangelical theology is by contrast often embedded in very unstructured and disordered worship with no liturgical pattern or flow. Contemporary evangelical worship is all too often highly individualistic and random, dependent on the whim of the leader or leaders and lacking clear form, objectivity or depth. It can also be highly manipulative and prescriptive. It seldom provides space or room for mystery and contemplation but rather a continuous, disordered, jarring assault on the senses.

I am a Presbyterian and I am conscious that Presbyterians are particularly keen on order – indeed we use the title Common Order rather than Common Prayer for our worship book. There are good reasons for this emphasis and they are well expressed in the preface to the most recent *Book of Common Order of the Church of Scotland*:

In worship we engage as the body of Christ in an encounter with Almighty God. This engagement should never become a rambling incoherence of well-meaning phrases and gestures. It should exhibit that deliberate and historical patterning of sentiment and expression which befits the meeting of the sons and daughters of earth with the King of Kings. Further, in public worship, as distinct from personal devotions it is important that the whole congregation sense a purpose and direction in their representation before God. They should never be placed in the position of being spectators at a performance which is entirely dependent on the aesthetic, emotional and spiritual whims of its leaders. This in no way precludes or denies the inspiration and direction of the Holy Spirit. The enemy of the Spirit is not form but anarchy.[11]

This ringing endorsement of the principle of order links it explicitly with the Holy Spirit, traditionally regarded in Christian theology as the third person of the Trinity. So it was for Augustine who saw creation taking place in three stages with the products of the first two stages, *modus* and *species*, presenting a world of isolated things that was given pattern and dynamic by the addition of *ordo*, the animating and governing force of the third person of the Trinity. For Augustine there was an intimate connection between order and peace and also between order and love. *Ordo Amoris* was, indeed, for him a key concept which incorporated not just the idea of a loving God but also the command to love our neighbours and ourselves which he found supremely expressed in the 'golden rule' at the beginning of the Sermon on the Mount. He was fond of quoting the prayer from the Song of Songs: '*Ordinate in me caritate*' (order in me love).[12]

In linking order, both as an attribute of God and as a mark of liberal theology, more specifically to the being and work of the second person of the Trinity, as I will be doing in this chapter, I am not seeking to deny or detract from the strong ordering qualities of both the first and third persons as they have traditionally been conceived. I propose this particular bracketing principally to emphasize both the understanding of Christ as the Logos, the Word made flesh, representing the creative principles of reason and order, and the Gospel portrayal of Jesus' life and ministry as being focused on wholeness, healing, integration and peace. The particular association of order with the person of Jesus Christ, the suffering servant, wounded healer and crucified one, establishes very clearly that order in this context is not about coercion and force but rather about humility and love.

Although I want to underline the particular relationship between Jesus Christ and order, I am well aware that in classic Christian theology, in the Bible and in the sacred texts of other faiths, order tends to be associated more generally with God. There are three broad dimensions to this understanding that are worth exploring in terms of the liberal theological approach that they encourage. First, it emphasizes a creative capacity and purpose continually bringing form, harmony and beauty out of nothingness, chaos and random, undifferentiated matter. The foundational creation myths of the Ancient Near East, from which the classic accounts in the Judaeo-Christian, Hindu and Islamic scriptures ultimately derive, view creation not as making matter but as ordering chaos. The world is seen as coming into being when God gains control of primordial chaos, usually represented by untamed water. Recent biblical scholarship tends to the view that this is also the perspective of the author of the first chapter of Genesis which portrays God creating order out of chaos rather than making the world out of nothing, or *ex nihilo*, a concept developed much later and first found in Jewish literature in II Maccabees, a work probably written in the second century before the birth of Jesus. In this original view, God's sovereignty is seen not in terms of the absolute origins of matter but in terms of establishing and preserving order. It provides a dynamic understanding of God's work in creation, focusing not just on the beginning of the world but on God's continuing work to sustain and preserve it.[13]

The emphasis in the opening of Genesis on the good ordering and fashioning of life out of chaos is echoed in Psalm 136 where thanksgiving for God's work at each stage of progressive creation – 'to him who by understanding made the heavens . . . who spread out the earth upon the waters . . . who made the great lights' – is accompanied by the refrain: 'for his steadfast love endures for ever'. As Jonathan Clatworthy observes: 'The Jewish scriptures describe the world as designed by a single benevolent being who intended it for the well-being of all creation and got it right. This view provides a conceptual framework for expecting the world to be ordered rather than chaotic. God intends *shalom* – peace, harmony, well-being and prosperity, for humans, animals and the land.'[14]

This same theme is evident in the Creation hymn of the Rig Veda, written between 1200 and 900 BC and one of the most sacred and normative of Hindu texts, which speaks of: 'He by whom the awesome sky and the earth were made firm, by whom the dome of the sky was propped up, and the sun, who measured out the middle realm of space' (10.121). It is there too in the Koran where there is a particular emphasis on balance, limitation, justice and equity, values which are all central to a liberal theological understanding of God's creative work and the response which it should elicit from us as creatures:

He created man and taught him articulate speech. The sun and the moon pursue their ordered course. The plants and the trees bow down in adoration. He raised the heaven on high and set the balance of all things, that you might not transgress that balance. Give just weight and full measure. He laid the earth for his creatures, with all its fruits and blossom-bearing palm, chaff-covered grain and scented herbs. He created man from potter's clay, and the jinn from smokeless fire. (Sura 55, 1–15)

This sense of ordered, purposeful creation coming out of chaos is beautifully expressed in some of the classic hymns from the eighteenth and nineteenth centuries:

> Thou, whose eternal word
> Chaos and darkness heard,
> And took their flight;
> Hear us, we humbly pray,
> And, where the Gospel day
> Sheds not its glorious ray,
> Let there be light!
>
> (J. Marriott, 'Thou, Whose Eternal Word'
> (original words), first verse)

> Before the hills in order stood,
> Or earth received her frame,
> From everlasting thou art God,
> To endless years the same.
>
> (I. Watts, 'O God, Our Help in Ages Past', third verse)

> O sacred spirit, who didst brood
> Upon the chaos dark and rude,
> Who bid its angry tumult cease
> And gave, for wild confusion, peace.
>
> (W. Whiting, 'Eternal Father, Strong to Save', third verse)

Each of these verses from well-known hymns contributes an important liberal element to the theological understanding of God as order. The first portrays God, or more specifically God's Word (and to that extent we can claim it as a Christological reference) as bringing enlightenment in place of darkness, an echo of the theme of the prologue of St John's Gospel discussed below. The second suggests the continuing nature of God's creative work – it is not a once-for-all activity but rather 'from everlasting thou art God, to endless years the same'. The third conveys a powerful sense of God as the one who gives peace instead of confusion, echoing Paul's great statement: 'God is not a God of confusion but of peace' (1 Corinthians 14.33). This last hymn also speaks powerfully and specifically of the ordering work of Jesus Christ, picking up the parables of the stilling of the storm and walking on the water which are seen in terms of bringing calm and peace out of rage and confusion:

> O Christ, whose voice the waters heard,
> And hushed their raging at thy word,
> Who walkedst on the foaming deep,
> And calm amid the storm didst sleep.
>
> ('Eternal Father, Strong to Save', second verse)

These three hymns, and the sacred texts on which they are based, speak strongly of divine steadfastness, faithfulness and ordered, measured purpose. They portray God as the still, stable centre representing calm, peace and order against wild confusion. It is a gentle, quiet understated calm rather than a heavy authoritarian hand, beautifully represented in the story of the word of God coming to Elijah, not in the wind, the earthquake or the fire but in the 'still, small voice' (1 Kings 19.11–12). There is something of the same feeling in the description of the day of Pentecost when the sound that comes from heaven 'like the rush of a mighty wind' is a prelude not to confusion but to order (Acts 2.2). In his poem, 'The Brewing of Soma', which compared the emotionalism whipped up in nineteenth-century American evangelical worship with the frenzied behaviour induced in some Hindus through the use of hallucinogenic drugs, John Greenleaf Whittier (1807–92) invoked the imagery of the story of God's appearance to Elijah to make a powerful plea for a liberal theological reading of the principle of order at the heart of God. What is striking about the two stanzas quoted below, which now form the closing verses of the abidingly popular hymn 'Dear

Lord and Father of Mankind', is not just the invocation of the still, small voice of calm but the prayer to 'let our ordered lives confess the beauty of thy peace'. This is not a piece of mushy sentimentalism, nor an injunction to quietism and withdrawal from the world, but rather, as one would expect from a serious and strenuous New England Quaker, a call to live more simply and mindfully in conformity with the teachings of Jesus and the ordered nature of God:

> Drop thy still dews of quietness,
> Till all our strivings cease;
> Take from our souls the strain and stress,
> And let our ordered lives confess
> The beauty of thy peace.
>
> Breathe through the heats of our desire
> Thy coolness and thy balm;
> Let sense be dumb, let flesh retire;
> Speak through the earthquake, wind and fire,
> O still, small voice of calm!

This brings us to the second and closely related aspect of seeing God in terms of order that has strongly influenced liberal theology: an emphasis on the pre-eminence of love in the work of creation and of continuing to hold together the world in harmony. Boethius followed Augustine in emphasizing the order of love which moves and animates the world:

> That the world can be trusted
> To turn in harmony,
> That opposite tendencies
> Keep everlasting pact,
> That Phoebus with golden disc
> Leads in the rosy day
> Till evening comes and Phoebe rules
> And night her laws obey;
> That the greedy sea must keep
> Her waves within their bounds

> Nor is earth allowed to stretch
> Beyond her broad expanse.
> All this procession of things,
> This earth and sky and sea
> Receives its order from love.[15]

It is easy but misleading to dismiss this elegant description of all creation 'receiving its order from love' as belonging to a long-defunct medieval world-view and having no relevance in our age of chaos theory and the uncertainty principle. A recent education workbook produced by the Church of England Board of Education juxtaposes what it presents as outmoded concepts like design, hierarchy, transcendence, depth, order and certainty with post-modern concepts such as chance, anarchy, immanence, chaos, openness, freedom and fallibility.[16] Such an exercise produces a false dichotomy. There is a range of values, including harmony, rhythm and balance, which stand between these two sets of extremes, and it is in them that the God of order is to be found. Order is an essential precursor of and adjunct to freedom. This is true among humans in the sphere of politics, religion and personal relations. Those who feel secure and at home in their own beliefs are most tolerant of and open to the beliefs of others. It is those who are insecure, feel threatened and lead disordered lives who are more likely to be fundamentalists. The same principle holds good in the physical world where many scientists increasingly see a balance of openness and order and are happy to use language which is not very different from that of Boethius:

> Nature's fixed order could not proceed on its path and the various kinds of change could not exhibit motions so orderly in place, time, effect, distance from one another, and nature, unless there was one unmoving and stable power to regulate them. For this power, whatever it is, through which creation remains in existence and in motion, I use the word which all people use, namely God.[17]

A prime contemporary exponent of such a perspective is Michio Kaku, a nuclear physicist and disciple of Stephen Hawking, who is seeking to complete Einstein's quest for a unified theory of everything. Kaku waxes eloquent about the deep harmony, structure and order in the world and says that modern physicists are not at all frightened of using the word 'God' to describe it:

> We use the word God in a different way from most religious people. Theirs is the God of intervention: the God that answers prayers, that walks on water and parts the Red Sea. Ours is the God of order and harmony, of physical law, of logic, the God of Einstein and Spinoza. There's harmony in the universe. When physicists talk about reading the mind of God, we mean reading the mind of order. It could have been chaos, but instead we have this infinite order that gets simpler and simpler as we get deeper and deeper.[18]

This is a highly significant statement. It underlines the extent to which contemporary physics, with all its acknowledgement of inherent instability and uncertainty in the make-up of the world, still posits an overall deep principle of order and harmony. It also reveals how a leading scientist is quite happy to label this principle 'God'. Kaku, in fact, explicitly invokes the prologue of St John's Gospel with its opening affirmation that in the beginning was the Word: 'To a physicist now, the Word is the quantum. So in the beginning was nothing, no time, no energy, Nirvana. There was no beginning or end. However, Nothing is unstable because of the quantum theory. So nothing must turn into something.'

This brings us to the third and perhaps most important and fruitful way in which God has been understood in terms of order, namely the doctrine developed from the prologue of John's Gospel of the Word or Logos as the central principle of creative order and reason. This Logos has been associated and identified specifically with Jesus Christ, the second person of the Trinity, and in John's words, the Word made flesh and dwelling among us. This is why I wish to identify order particularly with Christ and also why I think it is so important for liberal theology and its recovery. We might also point to two other key liberal themes which are contained in the Logos theology outlined in the prologue to John's Gospel. They are found together in its statement that with Jesus Christ's appearance on earth 'the true light that enlightens everyone was coming into the world' (John 1.9). This points both to the enlightening aspects of Christ as the Logos – he is the light that shines in the darkness – and also to the universality of his mission and reach – his light gives light to every human being and not just to a select or elect few. Both these aspects are well brought out, and linked to the healing and bringing of wholeness that characterized Jesus' earthly ministry, in the second Christological verse of the hymn, 'Thou, Whose Almighty Word':

> Thou who didst come to bring
> on thy redeeming wing
> healing and sight,
> health to the sick in mind,
> sight to the inly blind,
> now to all humankind,
> let there be light!

The Logos Christology expounded in the prologue to John's Gospel takes us back to Pablo Cassals' ideal of 'freedom with order'. For some strongly Trinitarian theologians like Raimundo Panikkar, it has suggested a continuing interchange in creation between the Logos representing form, order, shape and structure and the Spirit with its much freer role of constantly dissolving and re-forming all structures in endless movement. Others have been more drawn to the implications of the idea of ordered creation coming about *per verbum*, through the Word (and word) of God. For Timothy Ratcliffe, 'our story begins with God speaking a word, and Creation comes to be . . . The Word of God wells up from within human language. The birth pangs of the word started when the first human beings began to speak.' This linking of the Logos or primeval word of creation with the human capacity for speech leads Ratcliffe to propose that the coming of Jesus had to wait until language developed: 'Jesus could no more have been born earlier, then one could expect a baby Shakespeare to write *Hamlet*. The gestation of the Word took centuries.'[19] This suggestion that rational human discourse both echoes and partakes in the primal Word that ushered in creation gives extra force to the observation in the book of Proverbs that 'well ordered words are as a honeycomb, sweet to the soul and health to the bones' (Proverbs 16.24).

The essentially liberal implications of the understanding of Christ as the Logos were first worked out by the redoubtable Justin Martyr. For him, the Logos designated the Son in his cosmological function as the energetic Word of God (*logike dunamis*), the creator and organizer of the cosmos. Because the Word existed with God from the beginning, and before its specific incarnation in the world as Jesus Christ, its impact and influence are not confined to those who think of themselves as Christians. Everywhere there are people who have lived by the Word and so deserve to be called Christian:

> We have been taught that Christ is the first-begotten of God, and have testified that he is the Logos of which every race of humans partakes. Those who have lived in accordance with the Logos are Christians, even though they were called godless, such as, among the Greeks, Socrates and others like them; among the Barbarians, Abraham, Ananias, Azarias, Misael and Elijah, and many others, whose deeds and names I forbear to list.[20]

Justin Martyr goes on to make clear that what he means by living in accordance with the Logos is following the principles of reason, the dictates of conscience and the moral path. His is perhaps the earliest expression of what has come to be called the inclusivist position in terms of a Christian approach to those of other faiths – the belief that those living good lives by their own lights are in fact incorporated with Christ through the Logos and so come within the economy of salvation. What is especially important for liberal theology is the identification that Justin made between the Logos and the principle of reason. From Justin onwards, reason has been seen as central to the idea of the Logos. As we have already observed, it has also long been regarded as a key characteristic of liberal theology. Seeking to develop a liberal theology for the twenty-first century, Michael Langford echoes Justin's inclusivist Logos theology:

> Good persons by their actions, sincere scientists or scholars by their search for truth, and all artists who seek what is beautiful, to some degree and in their own way will find that they have sought God by responding to his *Logos*. Such a view leads inevitably to a

denial that only Christians or only monotheists have a place in the heart of God or in the glory of the world to come. No one comes to the Father except through the way that involves a response to what is seen as good or true or beautiful, because this is the way in which God's eternal word touches every person.[21]

For Langford, there are five ingredients which make reason the keystone of liberal theology: induction – 'an exercise of thinking in which different possibilities are balanced or weighed in a process that can be called judgment'; deduction – 'drawing particular conclusions from more general premises'; the rejection of authority as an adequate source of truth; the search for rational grounds for an overall position; and a final higher level which he sees being attained as 'the genius of finer minds enables leaps of imagination and reflection in order to see systems and hypotheses of new and seemingly strange kinds'.[22] This fifth ingredient takes us to the realm of the imagination and the non-rational and provides a welcome corrective to Langford's otherwise somewhat over-rational 'passion for reason' (see page 4).

The idea of Christ, the second person of the Trinity, as the Logos emphasizes the rational principle at the heart of God. Liberal theologians have celebrated the God of reason as much as the God of order. For the leading Cambridge Platonist, Benjamin Whichcote: 'Reason is the Divine Governor of man's life; it is the very voice of God.'[23] There is a further attribute to be added to this particular trinity and that is truth. The prologue to St John's Gospel describes the Word made flesh and dwelling among us as 'full of grace and truth'. This linkage of grace and truth is highly suggestive, as is the link made in the Vedic tradition in Hinduism between order and truth, seen as emerging together in the sacrificial fire of creation: 'Order and truth were born from heat as it blazed up' (*Rig Veda* 10.190). Jesus famously linked truth and freedom when he told his disciples, 'you shall know the truth and the truth will set you free' (John 8.32). This is a difficult text for liberals in some respects. It would have been more congenial, perhaps, had Jesus put it the other way around and anticipated Milton's great argument for free speech by saying, 'you shall know freedom and freedom will lead you to the truth'. Nonetheless, it is highly significant that he chose to link truth specifically with freedom. He could easily have said that knowing the truth would lead to certainty and sureness rather than to freedom.

What was the truth Jesus wished his hearers to grasp and that he told them would set them free? First and foremost it was the double realization of his status as the Son of God, and in John's terms therefore the eternal Word bringing enlightenment and full of grace and truth, and their own status as creatures of God, loved and affirmed, owing their existence to the purposeful and benevolent design of a creator. This second truth is shared by all the world's great faiths which agree in seeing some kind of ordered purpose and plan behind human life and the structure of the universe. The grasp of this metaphysical truth stands at the heart of all commitment to learning and knowledge. An overarching sense of order is in a very real sense the foundation of all the liberal disciplines practised in schools and universities which are as much the creation of the Islamic world as of Western Christendom. It lies at the heart of the pursuit of knowledge and the spirit of intellectual inquiry in which natural phenomena and human concepts alike can be studied because they are susceptible to classification, synthesis and connection.

There was another truth that Jesus wished his disciples to grasp and which he told them would make them free. This was to do with life and behaviour rather than belief, and specifically about the effects of turning aside from selfish lives and the slavery of sin and reorienting themselves as his followers to practise his gospel of selfless love and service. It takes us again to the crucial relationship between order and freedom, and specifically to the great paradox at the heart of the Christian gospel (and found in all of the other major faiths) that we are actually most free when we are liberated from the slavery of selfish desire. It is classically expressed in Christian terms in the opening phrase of the second collect for peace in the order for Morning Prayer in the *Book of Common Prayer*: 'O God, who art the author of peace and lover of concord, in the knowledge of whom standeth our eternal life, whose service is perfect freedom' and intensively explored by George Matheson in his hymn 'Make Me a Captive, Lord, and Then I Shall be Free'. It is spelled out particularly clearly in the sustained meditation on Christian freedom found in Paul's letter to the Galatians which begins with the ringing words, 'Christ set us free so that we should remain free' but later goes on to qualify the nature of this freedom: 'You were called to be free; only beware of turning your freedom into licence . . . instead, serve one another in love' (Galatians 5.13). The passage ends with that wonderful catalogue of liberal virtues which Paul lists as the fruits of the Spirit: 'love, joy, peace, patience, kindness, goodness, trustfulness, gentleness and self-control' (Galatians 5.22).

This reinforces a point which I have made already but which bears repetition. Liberalism in the theological as much as the political sphere is not about licence. It is rather a strenuous, selfless ethic which urges its adherents to live true to their high calling as free men and women made in the image of God, not slaves to self-indulgence and base appetites and desires. Writing about liberal Christianity, Martin Camroux notes that the key word in the Gospel is freedom, 'but it is not any old freedom. It is a freedom modelled on the freedom of Christ. And his was a freedom not for self but to choose the role of servant and slave. He used his freedom to give himself to others. For the Christian the fundamental freedom is not freedom to choose as an end in itself but the freedom to love.'[24] Liberal theology is not, as many of its conservative critics like to suggest, an ideology of 'anything goes' without boundaries or restraints. It does set limits to human appetites and inclinations towards greed and power, but it does so through the way of Jesus, by affirming people rather than berating them, calling them to lives of selfless service and seeking always to promote the principles of self-restraint, balance, limitation and harmony that together make up order.

There is, indeed, a close relationship between order and sacrifice, not least in terms of God's own self-giving. The medieval Jewish mystical movement known as the Kabbalah developed the idea of God emptying and limiting himself through and by the act of creation. One particular Kabbalistic mystic, Isaac Luria, who lived in the middle of the sixteenth century, used the word *zimsum*, meaning concentration or contraction, to describe the way in which God restricted and humbled itself in order to provide the empty space for creation to develop. The great contemporary reformed theologian Jürgen Moltmann has taken up this idea and linked it to the Christian doctrine of the self-emptying or *kenosis* of God through Christ who humbled himself and divested himself of his divinity to live and suffer alongside humanity.[25]

This is but one facet of the earthly Jesus as the bringer of order, integration, harmony and wholeness in a disordered and chaotic world. The Gospels portray Jesus interacting with humans to promote their physical, psychological and spiritual healing. In the stories of the nature miracles, like the stilling of the storm and walking on the water, they also portray him interacting with restless and disordered elements in the natural world. In the opinion of Carl Jung, this underlying commitment to integrative order even extended to Jesus' death on the Cross:

> The Cross signifies order as opposed to the disorderly chaos of the formless multitude. It is, in fact one of the prime symbols of order. In the domain of psychological processes it functions as an organising centre . . . The definition of the Cross or centre as the boundary of all things is exceedingly original, for it suggests that limits of the universe are not to be found in a non-existent periphery but in its centre. There alone lies the possibility of transcending this world.[26]

The creation myths of many religious traditions link order and sacrifice and often involve the sacrificial deaths of gods or god-like figures. We do not need to subscribe to theories of substitutionary atonement emphasizing punishment or propitiation to appreciate this connection. Indeed, these stories carry a very different message – it is the divine beings who are sacrificing, limiting and humiliating themselves in order to bring order and harmony. They serve as dark and troubling reminders of the cost of order and of liberty. For Christians, the event of the resurrection, representing a victory over the waste and decay of death, also brings order, as does the institution and celebration of the Eucharist in which Christ's broken body is remembered.

Without necessarily being apocalyptic, it is difficult to avoid the feeling that we live in a world which is increasingly disordered. The steady retreat from principles of order in the West over the last 50 years or so has, indeed, been one of main contributors to the collapse of liberal values. It has been charted by Francis Fukuyama in his 1997 Tanner Lectures published as a pamphlet entitled *The End of Order* and expanded in his 1999 book *The Great Disruption*. Fukuyama dates the collapse of social order from the mid-1960s, relating it to the decline of the institution of marriage, rising crime rates and the break-down of trust and the notion of self-sacrifice in favour of rampant individualism and immediate gratification. He is right to argue that social order is important to the future of liberal democracy. Genuine liberalism, the liberalism of grace, generosity and open-mindedness, cannot flourish without it. He is also right to point out that social order does not require or presuppose centralized authoritarianism and that it can flourish equally well if not better in decentralized communities. He calls for a reconstruction of values associated with a return to religiosity of a more liberal hue than previously in which 'religious belief is less an expression of dogma than of the community's existing norms and desire for order'.[27]

Culturally, too, there has been a clear retreat from order in favour of increasing brutalism, hedonism and commercialism, perhaps especially evident in the fields of music and architecture. The growing appeal of astrology and the occult and the proliferation of cults testify to an equally alarming flight from reason. We badly need a restoration of those values of order and harmony so well characterized in the *Bhagavad Gita*:

When a man dwells on the pleasures of sense, attraction for them arises in him. From attraction arises desire, the lust of possession, and this leads to passion, to anger.

From passion comes confusion of mind, then loss of remembrance, the forgetting of duty. From this last comes the ruin of reason, and the ruin of reason leads man to destruction.

But the soul that moves in the world of the senses and yet keeps the senses in harmony, free from attraction and aversion, finds rest in quietness.

The peace of God is with them whose mind and soul are in harmony, who are free from desire and wrath, who know their own soul.

(*Bhagavad Gita*, 2.62–65; 5.26)

These inner disciplines and qualities of awareness, mindfulness and restraint lie at the heart of liberalism and are essential to its reclamation. In his seminal book, *The Liberal Future*, Jo Grimond, the great British Liberal politician and thinker, identified the first principle of liberalism as responsibility. Second came a scepticism prepared to criticize without limits the most hallowed beliefs and institutions, and third a reliance on reason.[28] Unfortunately, self-centredness has come to serve as the default setting for so many at the expense of those other qualities commended in *Bhagavad Gita* and in the sacred texts of all the world's great faiths.

In the project to reclaim liberal theology, one of the most important tasks is enthusiastically to promote engagement between faith and knowledge and particularly between theology and science. Liberals can have no doubt that their answer to Tertullian's famous question, 'What has Athens to do with Jerusalem?', is 'A lot.' In the words of Raimundo Panikkar: 'God, as the foundation of the ordered relations of the world, is the ground of all intelligibility.'[29] God is to be approached and found through intellectual inquiry and reason as well as through prayer and faith. The fact that we believe we live in an ordered, intelligible, structured world means that we can and should study it. Bruno Guiderdoni, a devout Muslim scholar and director of the Lyon Observatory, says that as a Muslim he feels that the pursuit of scientific knowledge is a religious duty.[30]

There is a dangerously negative anti-scientific mentality abroad nowadays, fuelled especially by conservative evangelicals and fundamentalists but also encouraged by prominent Roman Catholics. It is taking us back to the mentality that set up the Inquisition and condemned Galileo. The relations between faith and scientific communities have not always been like this. Islam had very considerable respect for the advance of scientific knowledge in its early centuries. In the nineteenth-century heyday of liberal Protestantism, the companionship between science and religion was epitomized by the Victorian parson naturalists who combined pastoral ministry with serious and valuable research in the field of natural history. Typical was Leonard Jenyns, vicar of Swaffham Bulbeck in Cambridgeshire for 30 years. A devoted pastor and preacher, he was also a distinguished amateur naturalist, collecting more than 15,000 specimens of flowering plants and ferns. These two aspects of his life were held together by his overwhelming sense of the order of creation which he saw as a harmonious if exceedingly complex and diverse whole. As his biographer Patrick Armstrong comments, 'in his aspiration to live a good Christian life, and in his parish work alike, we see the love of order and decorum, the search for pattern, and a delight in the complexity of relationships unravelling before him'.[31]

Modern science offers exciting and encouraging messages and metaphors for contemporary theology, not least in its wonderfully dynamic view of the world. Recent advances in physics have shown that alongside chaos, indeterminacy and unpredictability there are underlying patterns of order and organization. The deterministic, utterly predictable world of Newtonian mechanics which underlay a certain kind of deism and design theory may be shattered, but it is still clear that within chaotic systems there are predictable scales and models. Chemistry and biology point to the phenomenon of self-organization whereby millions of molecules apparently spontaneously react and diffuse to set up highly complex and ordered spiralling shapes and patterns, in some respects reminiscent of interlacing Celtic knot-work. A new kind of music of the spheres is suggested by the discovery that all matter is vibrating energy. This gives a fresh slant to God's dynamic order, beautifully expressed in a prayer crafted by George MacLeod, founder of the Iona Community:

> In You all things consist and hang together:
> The very atom is light energy;
> The grass is vibrant,
> The rocks pulsate.
> All is in flux; turn but a stone and an angel moves.[32]

These and other scientific discoveries encourage a renewed natural theology where we look for and find God through creation as much as through revelation. Natural theology has always been a happy hunting ground for liberal theologians and it takes on a new urgency and imperative as we engage with climate change and the dramatic loss of species and biodiversity, considered in more detail in Chapter 6.

One of the most bizarre aspects of the anti-scientific mentality which conservative evangelical Christians have espoused is the galloping progress of creationism. This is particularly evident in the United States where some polls suggest that as many as two-thirds of the population now reject evolution in favour of creationism or intelligent design. Evolution does not seem to pose a problem for most adherents of other faiths – it is not a major issue in Islam, for example. As liberal theologians from the mid-nineteenth century onwards have argued, it should not pose a problem for Christians. It does admittedly point to an extremely high level of waste and suffering in the process whereby life has evolved and brings us back to the centrality of sacrifice. Evolution, however, is not fundamentally incompatible with the Genesis accounts of creation, read as a poetic and metaphorical answer to the question 'Why?' rather than a scientific account of how the world began. The Bible, in common with the sacred texts of all the major faiths, posits a movement from nothingness and undifferentiated, random chaos to ever higher levels of order, complexity and potential. The theory of evolution encourages us to view God less as a remote, authoritarian dictator supernaturally intervening to zap the world into being and more as the ground of all being with an intimate involvement in the continuing process of creation. God's purpose and presence are to be found not so much in miraculous interventions contrary to the laws of nature as in the evolutionary processes of nature itself. Process theology, associated with Alfred North Whitehead and Charles Hartshorne, in which God is seen as the self-surpassing surpasser, capable of change and development and luring creation on in love, provides one way of integrating theism and evolution that has appealed to several liberal theologians. It conceives of evolution as a series of 'falls upward' towards greater complexity, rejecting the idea of a single radical fall from a primeval state of perfection at the beginning of creation and locating the Garden of Eden as the ultimate destination rather than the starting point of the story.[33]

The media have hyped up the contemporary clash of religion and science, playing into the hands of the most strident and extreme voices on each side, and suggesting an inevitable incompatibility between faith and reason. The reality, as John Lennox has pointed out in his book, *God's Undertaker: Has Science Buried Religion?*, is that science is completely consistent with theism and in one key respect dependent on it, since theism provides an explanation for the intelligibility of the universe without which science cannot begin. Donald Hilton exposes the artificial conflict between reason and faith:

The debate is often conducted as though these were two separated and distinctly different steps to truth, and that to choose the one means the rejection of the other. Not so – they are two complementary ways in which we find faith; they interlock and need each other if we are to grasp the wholeness of the Gospel. We need both: mind and heart, thought and feeling, jumping from one to the other in our pilgrimage to truth.[34]

It is depressing to see mainstream churches and religious leaders opposing current scientific research, particularly when it is being pursued not just to forward knowledge but to advance the fight against debilitating illness and pain. Stem-cell research and the creation of hybrid embryos, combining human and animal DNA, have the potential to provide cures for terrible de-humanizing illnesses. Yet they have been opposed by many Christians. Most of the main British churches opposed the British Human Fertilization and Embryology Act passed in 2008. I believe that Gordon Brown was quite right to describe this measure, which had the backing of nearly all scientists and contained very careful checks and balances on the use of human embryos for research, as 'an inherently moral endeavour'. Stem-cell and embryo research deserves Christian support not just because it is at the cutting edge of science and medicine but principally because its purpose is to bring healing hope to those crippled by appalling illnesses and to their families who have to witness their suffering.[35] As has already been pointed out in the context of abortion, the main grounds for opposition by the churches – that human life begins with fertilization – is a relatively recent belief among Christians.

If an emphasis on order encourages a close relationship between theology and science, it also promotes a strong attachment to justice. This is clear from the way in which we talk about a new world order where structures and institutions embody values of peace and conflict resolution, human rights and the rule of law, fairer distribution and a more equal sharing of resources. These are the fundamental values shared by all the world's religions and by humanists as well, and which Jesus, who called them the values of the kingdom, taught and practised so clearly. Emphasizing order allies liberal theology inescapably and unequivocally with the search for a more just, equal and stable world.

It leads naturally to support for institutions like the United Nations – heralded by Attlee for uniting liberty and order – committed to the rule of law, the maintenance of human rights and to conflict resolution in the international sphere, and to active campaigning for disarmament, the relief of poverty, cancelling Third World debt, fair trade and the promotion of literacy, education and health care.

This point needs to be made with some force because liberalism is often associated today with unbridled capitalism and unregulated free-market economics. This is a travesty of true liberalism in any of its incarnations – theological, political, cultural, social or even economic. It is very unfortunate that a certain breed of modern conservative has hi-jacked the name neo-liberalism for a creed that is the antithesis of true liberalism, certainly as it has been understood in Britain. *Laissez-faire*, meaning unfettered free enterprise with the state leaving everything alone, has never really been a central part of the British liberal tradition nor the creed of the Liberal Party. The intervention of the modern state in industrial, social and economic questions began with the Liberal governments of the later nineteenth and early twentieth centuries. The 1907–10 Liberal government was arguably the most interventionist and redistributionist of any British administration.[36]

A renewed liberal theology based on the principle of order will have no truck with the rampant, unbridled, unregulated winner-takes-all capitalism that has arguably been the dominant religion of the last 30 years with its holy grail of continuing economic growth. It will attack the twin towers of greed and unaccountable power and challenge the idea that a nation or a people's well-being is measured principally by economic indicators such as gross domestic product and in terms of ever-growing wealth. It will rather laud the value of social capital, social cohesion, liberty, fairness and justice. It will champion those now rather neglected and despised virtues which are so essential to the orderly life of individuals and communities: commitment to public service and voluntary activity, honesty, integrity, reliability and responsibility.

I want to end this chapter by quoting from John Stuart Mill. He was not a liberal theologian – indeed he was not a religious believer and described himself in his *Autobiography* as one of the few examples in

Victorian Britain 'of one who has not thrown off belief but never had it'.[37] He was, however, an unmistakeable and foundational liberal thinker who was voted the greatest liberal ever by an overwhelming margin in a poll held at the 2007 British Liberal Democrat Party Assembly. One of his many passions which is highly relevant today was the stationary-state economy that he believed would and should emerge in the aftermath of capitalism. Economic growth, he argued, can only be temporary in a world of scarce resources in which the population constantly presses on land and food reserves. Unlike classical economists, he positively looked forward to a stationary economy because he believed that it would end the damaging effect on human character of the unremitting pursuit of possessions and the destructive consequences for the natural environment of open-ended economic growth.

> The best state for human nature is that in which, while no one is poor, no one desires to be richer, nor has any reason to fear being thrust back, by the efforts of others to push themselves forward . . . I know not why it should be a matter of congratulation that persons who are already richer than any one needs to be, should have doubled their means of consuming things which give little or no pleasure except as representatives of wealth . . . It is only in the backward countries of the world that increased production is still an important object: in those most advanced, what is economically needed is better distribution, of which one indispensable means is a stricter restraint on population.[38]

It is significant that Mill called for a restraint on population. This is surely one of the most urgent needs of our world now and is fully consonant with the principle of order that stands at the heart both of the being of God and of liberal theology. The huge explosion of world population is profoundly disordering environmentally, economically, socially and politically. Birth control is a cause that should engage faith groups passionately and positively. It is scandalous that a conservative coalition led by the Vatican and embracing fundamentalist Muslims, Mormons and Protestant evangelicals should be so vehemently opposing contraception and particularly the wider use and distribution of condoms.

Limitation on population is not enough. We also need limitation on lifestyles so that they become simpler and more mindful, less greedy and exploitative. Mill felt that a stationary state economy would give people 'sufficient leisure, both physical and mental from mechanical details, to cultivate freely the graces of life'.[39] Since his time the technological revolution has brought freedom from 'mechanical details', only to create a new kind of slavery and dependency culture. Meanwhile we have succumbed *en masse* to the illusion that the good life is measured primarily in terms of material advancement and conspicuous consumption despite the fact that rising affluence has signally failed to produce rising levels of well-being and satisfaction. The twin task of bringing life in all its abundance to those who are enslaved and impoverished in whatever way and of reversing our headlong rush towards ever more damaging and less sustainable economic growth is complex and daunting, but a commitment to order, God's good order, lies at the heart of it.

Notes

1. R. Eschbach, 'Der Geirekönig Joseph Joachim as Performer' (Lübeck: *Die Tonkust*, July 2007), p. 214.
2. I. Bradley, *The Celtic Way* (London: Darton, Longman & Todd, 1993), p. 2.
3. J. Begbie, *Theology, Music and Time*, p. 71.
4. R. Rastall, *The Heaven Singing: Music in Early English Religious Drama* (Woodbridge: Boydell & Brewer, 1996), p. 183.
5. D. Brown and A. Loades (eds), *The Sense of The Sacramental* (London: SPCK, 1995), p. 13.
6. I became acutely aware of the incompatibility between modern liberal hymns and many of the modern tunes written specially for them while singing the work of Fred Kaan and Brian Wren at the 'Free to Believe' Conference in 2008. The profoundly liberal sentiments of these two leading late-twentieth-century hymnwriters were much better brought out by using nineteenth-century tunes in the appropriate metre.
7. Inter-Faith Meeting, University of St Andrews Chaplaincy, 26 March 2009.
8. *Advices & Queries* (London: Society of Friends, 1997), p. 5.
9. Bradley 1992, p. 30.
10. 'A Living Tradition', *Church Music Quarterly* (June 2009), p. 33.
11. *Book of Common Order of the Church of Scotland* (Edinburgh: St Andrew Press, 1994), p. x.

12. On Augustine's concept of order, see J. Burnaby, *Amor Dei* (London: Hodder & Stoughton, 1938), pp. 113–37.

13. T. Hiebert, 'Genesis' in O'Day and Petersen 2009, p. 6.

14. Alker 2008, p. 61.

15. *De Consolatione Philosophiae*, translated by Mervyn Wilson, *Ecotheology* 10 (2001), p. 124.

16. *Tomorrow is Another Country: Education in a Post-Modern World* (London: Church House Publishing, 2004).

17. Boethius, *The Consolation of Philosophy*, trans. V. E. Watts (London: Penguin Books, 1969), sect. 3.12.

18. Interview, *Scotland on Sunday*, 22 October 1995, Spectrum section, p. 3. See Kaku's book *Hyperspace* (Oxford: Oxford University Press, 1995).

19. T. Ratcliffe, *Sacred Space: House of God and Gate of Heaven* (London: Continuum, 2007), pp. 65, 79.

20. Justin Martyr, First Apology, XLVI,1–4, quoted in Danielou (1973), pp. 40–1. On Justin's concept of the Logos, see J. Dupuis 2002, pp. 57 ff.

21. Langford 2001, pp. 187–8.

22. Langford 2001, pp. 16–18.

23. Powicke, *The Cambridge Platonists* (London: J. M. Dent, 1926), p. 48.

24. M. Camroux, *What is Best in Liberal Christianity* (*Free to Believe* pamphlet, n.d.), p. 7.

25. J. Moltmann, *God in Creation* (London: SCM Press, 1985), pp. 86–93. I explore this whole theme in much more detail in Bradley 1995, Chapter 2.

26. C. Jung, *Transformation Symbolism in the Mass*, quoted in R. A. Segal (ed.), *The Gnostic Jung* (London: Routledge, 1992), p. 119.

27. F. Fukuyama, *The Great Disruption* (London: Profile Books, 1999), p. 278.

28. J. Grimond, *The Liberal Future* (London: Faber, 1959), p. 12.

29. R. Panikkar, *The Trinity and the Religious Experience of Man* (1973), p. 48.

30. James Gregory Lecture, St Andrew's University, 9 October 2008.

31. P. Armstrong, *The English Parson Naturalist* (Leominster: Gracewing, 2000), p. 91.

32. G. MacLeod, 'Man is Made to Rise' in *The Whole Earth Shall Cry Glory: Iona Prayers* (Glasgow: Wild Goose Publications, 2007), p. 24.

33. On process theology, see J. B. Cobb and D. R. Griffin, *Process Theology: An Introductory Exposition* (1976). See also Bradley 1995, Chapters 2 and 8.

34. D. Hilton, *Where Reason Fails* (*Free to Believe* pamphlet, n.d.), p. 6.

35. See T. Peters, *Sacred Cells? Why Christians Should Support Stem Cell Research* (New York: Rowman & Littlefield, 2008).

36. See Bradley 1980.

37. J. M. Robson, *Collected Works of John Stuart Mill* (London: Routledge, 1963), Vol. I, p. 45.

38. J. S. Mill, *Principles of Political Economy* (Toronto: University of Toronto Press, 1965), Vol. II, pp. 754–5.

39. Mill 1965, p. 755.

5

Openness

Openness is a value dear to the liberal heart, and liberal theology is often categorized as open theology. This openness can be expressed in many different ways. Jürgen Moltmann expresses his 'theology of hope' in terms of an open future which he sums up as the 'not yet' dimension of both God and human existence. In a very different vein, W. H. Vanstone wrote in his classic book of 'the stature of waiting', that state of openness and receptivity which he saw as characterizing Jesus throughout his passion. I myself have used the metaphor of pilgrimage to suggest a theology which is on the way and not yet arrived, embracing and absorbing ambiguities, doubts and hopes.[1]

In his book *Religion and Revelation*, Keith Ward lists what he sees as the essential features of open theology:

1. It will seek a convergence of common core beliefs, clarifying the deep arguments which may underlie diverse cultural traditions.
2. It will seek to learn from complementary beliefs in other traditions, expecting that there are forms of revelation one's own tradition does not express.
3. It will be prepared to reinterpret its beliefs in the light of new, well-established factual and moral beliefs.
4. It will accept the full right of diverse belief systems to exist, as long as they do not cause avoidable injury or harm to innocent sentient beings.
5. It will encourage a dialogue with conflicting and dissenting views, being prepared to confront its own tradition with critical questions arising out of such views.
6. It will try to develop a sensitivity to historical and cultural contexts of the formulation of its own beliefs, with a preparedness to continue developing new insights in new cultural situations.

Ward also lists the characteristics of closed theology:

1. It insists on the total distinctiveness of its own beliefs, excluding others from any share in important truths.
2. It rejects contact with other systems of belief.
3. It rejects any developments of knowledge which would force a reinterpretation of its own tradition.
4. It will, if possible, restrict or prevent the expression of criticism or dissent.
5. It will seek to suppress other religions.
6. It will insist that it possesses a complete or sufficient understanding of truth, which change could only impair or destroy.[2]

In keeping with the overall shape and structure of this book – and here order is rearing its head again – I want to posit openness both as one of the essential attributes of God and as being related especially to the role and working of the Holy Spirit, traditionally seen in Christianity as the third person of the Trinity. Openness is also a very clear characteristic of Jesus, in both his life and teaching, and I certainly do not want to suggest that it is restricted to the Spirit. However, it does seem to me that openness is in a very distinct and definite way the particular property of the Spirit. This is represented biblically in the portrayal of the coming of the Spirit at Pentecost as being like the rush of a mighty wind (Acts 2.2) and in the statement in John's Gospel: 'the wind blows where it wills, and you hear the sound of it, but do not know whence it comes or whither it goes; so it is with everyone who is born of the Spirit' (John 3.8). As Raimundo Panikkar puts it, 'the Spirit is freedom, the freedom of Being to be what it is'.[3] Associating theological liberalism with the workings of the Spirit, as I also wish to do in this chapter, picks up on this theme of freedom and also emphasizes that liberalism is a matter of the spirit – a frame of mind, an outlook, a gut feeling – rather than a system or set of propositions. Kenneth Cauthen writes of 'the "liberal spirit" – that flexible temper of mind, openness to new truth, broad minded toleration of differences of opinion, and spirit of humility which has been characteristic of liberal thinking'.[4]

The association of the Spirit with the themes of wind and freedom has been pursued particularly effectively in song. I often begin my Pentecost sermons by reciting the open-ended questions in Bob Dylan's 'Blowing in the Wind'. Margaret Old's 'Spirit of God, Unseen as the Wind, Gentle as is the Dove', set to the tune of the Skye Boat Song, catches the gentleness and elusiveness of the Spirit, while Damian Lundy's 'The Spirit Lives to Set us Free, Walk, Walk in the Light' combines the themes of liberation and enlightenment. For me, the hymn that best expresses the Spirit's unpredictable openness and its power to blow away our stale prejudices is Cecily Taylor's 'The Bright Wind of Heaven' with its invitation 'So lean on the wind, it will show us the way'. The author, who has herself made a pilgrimage from Anglicanism through Congregationalism to her present home in the Society of Friends, wrote it in the early 1970s, 'triggered off by thoughts of the Spirit's movements both within and outside the churches'. In her words, 'the text refers to the widest possible movements of the Spirit wherever there is love or justice in our world'.[5]

> The bright wind is blowing, the bright wind of heaven,
> And where it is going to, no one can say;
> But where it is passing our hearts are awaking
> To stretch from the darkness and reach for the day.
>
> The bright wind is blowing, the bright wind of heaven
> And many old thoughts will be winnowed away;
> The husk that is blown is the chaff of our hating,
> The seed that is left is the hope of our day.
>
> The bright wind is blowing, the bright wind of heaven,
> The love that it kindles will never betray;
> The fire that it fans is the warmth of our caring,
> So lean on the wind, it will show us the way.[6]

The quality of openness, and especially openness to the future, is not just associated with the Spirit in Christian theology but is also a fundamental characteristic of God. The Judaeo-Christian understanding of creation affirms that rather than clinging to self-sufficiency, God opens a space for otherness, for matter and life to thrive in their diversity. As portrayed in the Bible, God is of the future as much as, if not more than, of the present, the one who is always ahead of us and who lures us on into the uncertainty, the possibility and the potentiality of what is to come. Translations do not always bring this out. The words God says to Abraham following the revelation in the burning bush, usually rendered as 'I am who I am', have a future orientation in the original Hebrew and would be more accurately rendered in English as 'I will be who I will be' (Exodus 3.14). A similar sense of the God of the future travelling ahead of his people is conveyed in descriptions of the Israelites wandering through the wilderness: 'By a pillar of cloud thou didst lead them in the day, and by a pillar of fire in the night to light for them the way in which they should go' (Nehemiah 9.12). The central motif of the Exodus experience is of God leading his people on to an open future. This theme carries on through and until the end of the New Testament when the Holy One declares: 'Behold I have set before you an open door, which no one is able to shut' (Revelation 3.8).

This emphasis on openness is fundamental to the concept of salvation as it is expressed in the Hebrew word *Yasha* from which the name 'Jesus', understood as 'he who saves', is derived. *Yasha* means to become wide or spacious – its opposite, *sara*, means to be narrow – and it came to mean rescuing people from being confined and restricted. Psalm 74 uses the word *Yasha* to describe God's work in creation liberating and ordering formless matter. There is a theme running through the Old Testament of God making people's lives broader and more spacious: 'the Lord in majesty will be for us a place of broad rivers and streams' (Isaiah 33.21). Unfortunately the Greek word *soteria* which came to be used for salvation in the Christian context has very different connotations. Rather than emphasizing liberation from a cramped and narrow existence it means deliverance from imprisonment in the physical body and rescue from the burden of material existence. Sadly, this has become a prominent theme in Christianity, with the attendant consequences of an obsession with sexuality and a strong conviction that the physical is evil. We need to recover the Hebrew idea of salvation implicit in the term *Yasha* as liberation from all that cramps and impedes life in place of the narrow concentration on saving souls from damnation that goes with *soteria*.[7]

Jesus' statement, 'I came that they might have life and have it abundantly' (John 10.10), is in keeping with this concept of *Yasha*, emphasizing positive rather than negative freedom, making life more wide and spacious rather than restricting and cramping it. There is a similar emphasis in his words, 'We piped for you and you did not dance', where he seems to be willing his followers to be more liberated and joyful (Matthew 11.17–19, Luke 7.31–35). These are among many occasions recorded in the Gospels where Jesus preaches and practises open theology and radical inclusiveness. It is striking how the times when he is portrayed as becoming angry are so often when people are being excluded or exclusive. He reprimands the disciples for trying to stop children being brought to him and the priests and the scribes for seeking to exclude children from the temple (Matthew 19.13–14, 21.15). He is annoyed with the Pharisees and 'grieved at their hardness of heart' when their narrow legalism causes them to criticize him for curing a man with a withered hand on the Sabbath (Mark 3.1–6).

Jesus' preferred method of putting his message across was through open-ended parables, stories, riddles and questions rather than dogmatic assertions and lectures. He taught through dialogue rather than monologue. He encouraged those he met to work out their own answers and come to their own conclusions. He often left them guessing and pondering and seemed almost deliberately to lead them into ambiguity. Whether talking to a woman caught in the act of adultery or to the Roman governor of Judea, he responded to simple and straightforward questions with a cryptic phrase or by himself asking a question. Again and again, he kept conversations going and kept them open-ended instead of closing them down with a pat answer. Donald Hilton illustrates and illuminates the technique in this para-phrase and reflection on the conversation that leads up to the story of the Good Samaritan:

Lawyer	What must I do to inherit eternal life?
Jesus	You tell me. What does the law say?
Lawyer	Love the Lord your God and your neighbour.
Jesus	Grand! You've got it right first time. Congratulations.
Lawyer	But who is my neighbour?
Jesus	Let me tell you a story so you can work it out for yourself.

> This is not a dogmatist eager to impose a creed and wanting to feed
> the right answer to people. It is the liberal, open-ended teacher
> more concerned that people should think and grow, than that they
> should get ten out of ten and a gold star for getting everything
> right.[8]

Jesus is portrayed by the Synoptic Gospel writers as himself being on a
perpetual journey, both physically and in other respects. He developed
his own mind and shaped his thoughts by listening and responding
to what others said. This is most dramatically evidenced in his extra-
ordinary encounter with the Canaanite woman where her vehement
arguments apparently led him to change his mind (Matthew 15.21–28).
He encouraged people to assume the attitude of seekers and pilgrims,
promising them: 'Ask and it will be given you; seek, and you will find;
knock and it will be opened to you' (Matthew 7.7, Luke 11.10). Once
again, the translation of this statement found in most Bibles does not
do justice to the tense of the original Greek verbs, which is present continuous. It should really read, 'Go on asking and it will be given you; go
on seeking and you will find; go on knocking and it will be opened to
you.' Jesus is calling here for a constant spirit of openness on the part of
his followers, and at the same time he is, in the true spirit of *Yasha*, presenting himself as the one who will open the door to them.

In deliberately reaching out beyond his comfort zone and making
himself especially available to the poor, the prostitutes, the sick, lepers
and children, Jesus incarnates the openness and availability of God,
who relates to his people not through certainty of belief and loyalty to
narrow religion but through openness to others in all their differences.
Reflecting on this open approach, Graham Hellier writes:

> It is difficult to envisage that Jesus sought to found a 'religion' or
> establish 'Christianity'. He spoke of God's kingdom and lived it; he
> looked for sincerity, faith and compassion in all kinds of people.
> He questioned narrow prejudice and established religion. He
> taught his followers to hearken to the free spirit of God who works
> without constraint. He did not provide a creed or a catechism but
> asked us to live by faith.[9]

A further important dimension to Jesus' openness is highlighted in his words to his disciples following the Last Supper in John's Gospel: 'I have yet many things to say to you, but you cannot bear them now. When the Spirit of truth comes, he will guide you into all the truth' (John 16.12–13). This is a remarkable statement, surely impossible to read other than in terms of the idea of progressive revelation. It brings us to another crucial if much neglected role of the Spirit, variously described in John's Gospel as the Counsellor and the Spirit of truth, as the one whom Jesus promises that the Father will send in his name to teach all things. His promise suggests very strongly that the New Testament is not the last word from God and that there is more to be revealed. This has been a persistent theme of liberal theologians down the centuries. It was classically expressed by John Robinson, the English Separatist pastor, when he preached to members of his exiled congregation as they left Leyden in the Netherlands in July 1620 on their way to England and thence to the New World on the *Mayflower*. In his parting words, he told this group, who went on to land at Plymouth, Massachusetts and are remembered as the true Pilgrim Fathers, to be ready to receive anything that God should reveal to them by any other instrument, as they were to receive any truth by his own ministry, 'for he was very confident that the Lord had more light and truth yet to break forth out of his holy word'. Robinson's words are amplified in a nineteenth-century hymn by George Rawson:

> We limit not the truth of God
>   To our poor reach of mind,
> By notions of our day and sect,
>   Crude, partial, and confined:
> No, let a new and better hope
>   Within our hearts be stirred:
> *The Lord hath yet more light and truth*
> *To break forth from His word.*[10]

A recent poster campaign by the United Church of Christ entitled 'God is still speaking' vividly illustrates this theme with its logo of a large comma and a quotation from the American comedian Grace Allen: 'Never place a period (full stop in English usage) where God has placed a comma.' Contemporary liberal theologians argue that God's revelation is progressive and continuing. Discussing John 16.12, Bishop Gene Robinson asks: 'Could it be that God revealed in Jesus Christ everything possible in a first-century Palestine setting to a rag-tag band of fishermen and working men? Could it have been God's plan all along to reveal more and more of himself and his will as the church grew and matured? Could it be that even the Bible is too small a box in which to enclose God?'[11] God's communication with humanity did not cease with the writing of the New Testament and the closing of the canon of scripture. It continues through history, into the present and beyond into the future. As Graham Hellier puts it, 'To believe in the continuing work of the Spirit is to acknowledge a progressive Gospel. It is therefore wholly misleading to set up an opposition between fresh insights over against those of scripture and tradition. The former is not human wisdom rearing itself against God's wisdom as though God shut up shop two thousand years ago.'[12]

Viewed in the light of continuing revelation and of his own promise, 'When the Spirit of truth comes, he will guide you into all the truth', Jesus' statement, 'You shall know the truth and the truth shall make you free', discussed in the previous chapter (page 87), takes on a new and broader perspective. So does his other saying about the truth recorded in John's Gospel and so often cited as a proof text for Christian exclusiveness: 'I am the way, the truth and the life; no one comes to the Father, but by me' (John 14.6). Many scholars now regard this as a Johannine interpolation provoked by particular divisions within the Church at the time this Gospel was written. But even if we take it at face value as a genuine saying of Jesus, his self-description does not necessarily carry a closed, exclusivist meaning. The truth is one of a trinity of attributes that Jesus ascribes to himself which overall suggest openness. This is certainly the case with his description of himself as the way, with its connotations of journeying and seeking, and the life with its message of abundance, vitality and energy. If Jesus is saying here that no one comes to the Father other than by his way, then that is the way of openness and vulnerability. The truth in this context is not an intellectual proposition but rather the embodiment in human life of the true character of God, wide and spacious in his mercy and grace. In the words of Edward Schillebeeckx, 'the God of Jesus is a symbol of openness, not closedness'.[13]

What indeed does truth mean in the context of these two familiar sayings of Jesus, and indeed in the broader context of liberal theology? First and foremost it means a work in progress, something which is never complete or closed but always open to new insights and interpretations. This is what Jesus himself seems to suggest in his remarks about the future activities of the Spirit in leading people into truth. It is also what Paul seems to be saying in his famous words, 'now we see through a glass darkly; but then face to face. Now I know in part; but then shall I know even as I also am known' (1 Corinthians 13.12). Here is a clear testimony to the tentative and evolving nature of truth and our partial grasp of it. In this world at least, we will never have the whole truth, and we will certainly never have it to ourselves. Truth can only be glimpsed and never possessed. Its pursuit is a continuing, shared journey of discovery. Proceeding with the best methods we have, all that we can hope to arrive at are limited provisional truths. We are always looking ahead for truth that is to be fully known in forms as yet unknown. This journey is at the very heart of liberal theology. The New Testament scholar James Dunn observes that 'liberalism encapsulates the lasting insight that all our knowledge is incomplete, all expressions of truth are fallible and corrigible'.[14]

To pursue truth involves constant questioning. It is indeed about 'living the questions', to use the title adopted by the liberal alternative to the Alpha course (see page 167). It is to follow the way that Jesus lived and taught, and in which God responded to Job in the most sustained divine–human dialogue in the Hebrew Bible. It is pre-eminently the Jewish way of seeking truth – the way of argument and debate, including argument with God, acknowledging and revelling in ambiguity and paradox – well summed up by Jonathan Sacks:

Truth on earth is not, nor can it aspire to be, the whole truth. It is limited, not comprehensive; particular, not universal. When two propositions conflict, it is not necessarily because one is true and the other false. It may be, and often is, that each represents a different perspective on reality, an alternative way of structuring order. In heaven there is truth; on earth there are truths.[15]

Approaching truth through paradox, by putting two contradictory statements side by side, was also the way of the Greek Church Fathers, of Dionysius the Areopagite and John Scotus Eriugena. It is not peculiar to the Judaeo-Christian tradition, and finds frequent expression in Hinduism. The creation hymn from the *Rig Veda* piles question upon question in its account of the creation, deliberately throwing up puzzles and challenges, paradoxes and unanswerable questions, and ending on a distinctly uncertain note on the subject of divine omniscience:

> Who really knows? Who will here proclaim it? Whence was it produced? Whence is this creation? Who then knows whence it has arisen? Perhaps it formed itself, or perhaps it did not – the one who looks down on it, in the highest heaven, only he knows – or perhaps he does not know. (*Rig Veda* 10.129, verses 6, 7)

As well as relishing questioning, ambiguity and paradox, liberal, open theology also values doubt and uncertainty. Jonathan Clatworthy observes that 'the willingness to accept uncertainty characterises religious liberals'.[16] For the liberal believer, the opposite of faith is not doubt but rather certainty. Certainty does not need faith because certainty knows. Indeed, it knows so well that it does not need to ask any more questions. The one who knows all the answers is literally faith-less. In Donald Hilton's words, 'such a one has stepped out of the pilgrimage because the deafening answers have destroyed the whispered questions . . . certainty has closed eyes and ears'.[17] Once again, Paul put it well when he said 'we walk by faith, not by sight . . . hope that is seen is not hope. For who hopes for what he sees?' (2 Corinthians 5.7, Romans 8.24). The great Christian virtues of faith and hope are about trusting where there is no clarity or certainty. To have faith is to live in what the anonymous thirteenth-century English medieval mystic called 'the cloud of unknowing'. There is a whole tradition in Christian theology based on not knowing rather than knowing. It is called the apophatic tradition and it approaches God on the basis of God's essential unknowability. It is particularly characteristic of Eastern Christian thought and goes back to Origen, Clement of Alexandra and Gregory of Nyssa who argued that not only is the essence of God unknowable but so also is the essence of even such a tiny creature as the ant. Gregory viewed the Christian life as a progression through the stages of purification and illumination to the highest stage in which the soul, longing more and more for God, realizes God's utter unknowability and is lost in the divine darkness. Donald Hilton gives a modern and distinctively liberal interpretation to this tradition:

> By liberal I mean that in my Christian faith there is a not-knowing as well as a knowing. It is too big for me to comprehend. Simultaneously, I walk in the light and in the darkness, and I call that ambivalence 'faith'. It is not that I sometimes have faith and sometimes lose faith but rather that what we normally call 'assurance' and what we normally call 'doubt' are both elements of a mature faith . . . any definition of faith that even began to satisfy me would have to include the assumption that faith involves the call to live confidently in uncertainty.[18]

The important role played by doubt in faith and in coming to truth is beautifully expressed by John Donne, another of those seventeenth-century English divines who are perhaps the true fathers of liberal theology, in his poem 'Satyre III: Of Religion':

> Doubt wisely, in strange way
> To stand inquiring right, is not to stray;
> To sleep, or run wrong, is; on a huge hill
> Cragged and steep, Truth stands, and he that will
> Reach her, about must, and about must go;
> And what the hill's suddenness resists, win so.[19]

If the liberal mind finds truth by doubting wisely, it is also open to science and developments in the field of human knowledge and is ready to change, modify and accommodate its beliefs in the light of new discoveries and insights. There is a striking visual expression of this openness in the sculptures over the west portal of the interdenominational Riverside Church in New York built in 1930 for the great liberal preacher Harry Emerson Fosdick after fundamentalists forced him out of his ministry in First Presbyterian Church in Fifth Avenue. Alongside Luther, Calvin and Wesley are statues of Muhammad,

Buddha, Confucius and a group of scientists including Darwin and Einstein. They were put there because Fosdick believed that all new truth, whoever its human agents, comes from God and should be welcomed in the Church.

Liberal theology is not just open to science and new intellectual discoveries. It is also open to mystery. Liberals are often accused of being over-rational and of over-intellectualizing faith. In fact, there are close affinities between liberal and mystical theology. Both point to the essential unknowability of a God who is to be approached through open awareness, contemplation and love rather than through propositional and dogmatic statements. We come back here to the primacy of grace in liberal theology and to a point that is well expressed in *The Cloud of Unknowing*:

> But now you will ask me, 'How am I to think of God himself, and what is he?' and I cannot answer you except to say 'I do not know!' For with this question you have brought me into the same darkness, the same cloud of unknowing where I want you to be! God may well be loved, but not thought. In love he can be caught and held but by thinking never.[20]

Authentic open liberal theology embraces mystery, spiritual experience, truths that are beyond words and that are embodied in ritual and tradition. It has that open, imaginative mysticism found in the prayers of George MacLeod:

> Invisible we see You, Christ beneath us.
> With earthly eyes we see beneath us stones and dust
> And dross, fit subjects for the analyst's table.
> But with the eye of faith, we know You uphold.[21]

It is very important that this aspect of liberal theology is reclaimed alongside the commitment to reason with which it is more often associated. Martin Camroux is absolutely right to insist that 'liberalism begins with a sense of the mystery of life and the inadequacy of our understanding'.[22] As we have noted, the mystical, experiential emphasis of Schleiermacher and the Romantics was an important influence on modern liberal theology. Jaroslav Pelikan identifies the importance of this strain in the American liberal theological tradition: 'American religious liberalism believed, with its mentors, Schleiermacher and Rudolf Otto, that a part of the uniqueness of religious faith was to be found, not in a sacred sub-species of intellectual knowledge nor yet in the moral life as such, but in the experience of the Holy.'[23] Openness to mystery brings believers from different traditions closer together. Doctrinal points may divide, but religious experience can bridge gaps and forge deeper alliances across faiths. The mystic Evelyn Underhill rightly observed that 'religions meet where religions take their source, in God'.

Standing alongside a commitment to reason and advances in the field of human knowledge and discovery, openness to mystery and wonder also allies theology more closely with modern science. It is striking how many scientists today use religious and poetic language to describe their findings, especially at the frontiers of physics, astronomy and biology. The close relationship between scientific endeavour and liberal theology noted in the previous chapter in the context of order is also evident in a shared commitment to openness. Describing his own journey into liberal theology, Donald Hilton notes: 'It was the insights of science that gave my pilgrimage that sense of openness to new truth which has made me a liberal in religious understanding.'[24] The fact is that liberal theology is open to reason, science and new intellectual insights and also to wonder, mystery and the cloud of unknowing. The combination and convergence of these two streams is the subject of a hymn by Tom Troeger, which underlines the importance of holding on to reason and learning while not losing our sense of wonder and mystery.

> Praise the source of faith and learning
> Who has sparked and stoked the mind
> With a passion for discerning
> How the world has been designed.
> Let the sense of wonder flowing
> From the wonders we survey
> Keep our faith forever growing
> And renew our need to pray.

God of wisdom, we acknowledge
That our science and our art
And the breadth of human knowledge
Only partial truth impart.
Far beyond our calculation
Lies a depth we cannot sound
Where your purpose for creation
And the pulse of life are found.

May our faith redeem the blunder
Of believing that our thought
Has displaced the grounds for wonder
Which the ancient prophets taught.
May our learning curb the error
Which unthinking faith can breed
Lest we justify some terror
With an antiquated creed.

As two currents in a river
Fight each other's undertow
'Til converging they deliver
One coherent steady flow.
Blend, O God, our faith and learning
'Til they carve a single course
While they join as one returning
Praise and thanks to you their source.[25]

The sense of being open to future possibility and potentiality is also present in liberal Islam where it is expressed in the idea of keeping open the door of *ijtihad*. For Muhammad Iqbal (1877–1938), perhaps the most influential liberal Muslim in the twentieth century and widely considered the spiritual father of Pakistan, the essence of Islam is evolutionary change and movement.[26] This outlook accords with the direction and emphasis of much modern science and philosophy where the old notion of a predetermined, mechanical world has given way to the much more open possibilities and intrinsic unpredictabilities suggested by quantum physics and Werner Heisenberg's uncertainty principle. Karl Popper, the philosopher perhaps most associated with the concepts of the open future and the open society, has suggested that the old world-view of 'the past kicking us and driving us with kicks into the future' can no longer be sustained in a world of indeterminacy and uncertainty. Rather, we should think in terms of possibilities, even possibilities that have not yet realized themselves, which he regards as constituting a reality in the making:

> In so far as these possibilities can, and partly will, realise themselves in time, in the future, the open future is almost as a promise, as a temptation, as a lure present, indeed actively present, at every moment . . . It is not the kicks from the back, from the past, that *impel* us, but the attraction, the lure of the future and its attractive possibilities that *entice* us: this is what keeps life – and, indeed, the world – unfolding. The future is open.[27]

Many physicists now see the intrinsic unpredictability revealed by quantum physics as revealing the openness of the world to its future rather than exposing an underlying indeterminacy or chaos. For theists, this accords well with a view of God as having a future orientation, the one who is ahead of us and says, 'I will be what I will be.' Process theology regards change and movement as the fundamental reality and God as part of that process and not standing outside it (see page 94). Notable contemporary Christian scientists like John Polkinghorne and Arthur Peacocke speak of God interacting with the world in such a way as to give it both regularity and an openness to its future and describe creation as being more like an unfolding musical improvization than a fixed score.[28]

Where is there a need for more openness in contemporary theology and church life? First, in our understanding of and approach to God. We need, in Denis Diderot's phrase, to *Elargissez Dieu*, to 'make God bigger', or perhaps more accurately to open our minds to expand our concept of the divine. In the words of a hymn by Andrew Pratt:

> How can we confine
>   God within our mind,
> Held within a creed
>   Humanly designed?
>
> How can we be sure
>   That the way we know
> Is the only path
>   That this God might show?[29]

Second, we could do with much greater openness in the way in which we read and interpret the scriptures. As well as the insights of biblical criticism, contextual studies and other tools being applied by academic biblical scholars, we need imagination, empathy and an understanding that, in the words of Krister Stendhal, former Dean of Harvard Divinity School, the Bible is 'not history minus but poetry plus'. The role of the Spirit here is crucial. Keith Ward has helpfully pointed to the fact that all scripture is God-breathed, or *theopneustos* as it is put in 2 Timothy 3.16, but not God-dictated. He draws an analogy with the spirit or breath of God sweeping over the waters of the formless void at creation. 'So when scripture is God-breathed, it becomes, by the action of the Spirit, a source of life and wisdom. That does not mean that God actually dictated it, so that there are no human errors or no different points of view or no developments of understanding in the text.' Quoting Romans 7.6, Ward urges us to read the Bible in the knowledge that 'we serve in the new way of the Spirit, and not in the old way of the written code'.

> It is in the new way of the Spirit in which we live, and all written codes, including that the Bible, must be judged, and sometimes found wanting, by the test of whether they point to the liberation of new life in the Spirit, or rather to the bondage of some written code, even if it is in the Bible itself, from which Christ has set us free.[30]

The spread of the relatively modern fundamentalist doctrines of inerrancy and literalism have spread darkness rather than light in terms of appreciation and understanding of the scriptures. They have encouraged a view of the Bible as a closed rather than an open book and have limited and boxed God into its pages. William Sloane Coffin sagely observed that 'the fundamentalist uses the Bible as a drunk uses a lamp post, for support not illumination'. In a blog written during the 2008 Lambeth Conference, Martin Shaw, former Bishop of Argyll and the Isles in the Scottish Episcopal Church, reflects that when he was a theological student in the 1960s, 'the Bible was seen as a highly complex piece of literature that revealed in varying and sometimes in conflicting ways the story of liberation of a people'. Its complexity demanded that those undergoing training for priesthood must take seriously literary analysis and criticism and the considerable uncertainty about who was involved in the creation of the writings and for what and for whose purpose they were written. He continues: 'For me that uncertainty adds to the adventure and importance of the Bible about which there is always a question mark. Sadly, much of that critical approach to the Bible has disappeared. I feel that there is a Christian mentality now that wants little else but certainties, and truth is in danger of being a casualty.'[31] The growing trend towards more closed literal readings of sacred texts is of course by no means confined to Christians. It is a major feature of modern Islam and there is a vital need for a more open and critical approach to the Koran. This makes the statement by Imam Muhammad Ashafa that 'scriptures have metaphorical as well as literal meanings' all the more important.[32]

Third, we need a greater openness to the past. As Karl Barth observed, this is just as important an aspect of having truly liberal openness to the future. In discussing, I have already suggested that one of the main contributory causes of the present crisis in liberal theology is the decoupling of theology from history in favour of philosophy (page 35). Historical consciousness and an appreciation of the value of tradition is, or should be, a hallmark of the open liberal mind. John Killinger is absolutely right to say that 'The prejudiced liberal mind, which cannot bear to hear and see what is traditional, is no more liberated than the prejudiced conservative mind that cannot tolerate what is novel or unconventional. The true liberal, the free man in Christ, ranges easily through time (past and present) and space (secular and holy).'[33]

Fourth, the Christian churches, and indeed all faith communities, could do with more of a sense of themselves as pilgrims and seekers. In my book on the state of churches in Britain in the 1990s, I distinguished two kinds of Christians – the pilgrims and the marchers:

> The pilgrims continue on their quest, welcoming others as companions on a journey that has many twists and deviations. The marchers have a much clearer sense of their destination and a greater certainty that they have already reached it. They also believe that there is only one route and feel an overwhelming compulsion to bring everyone else with them along it.[34]

Today there are still many marchers around, dogged, dogmatic, their eyes not looking around in wonder and expectation but fixed determinedly straight ahead or cast down to the ground. But there are also more and more pilgrims, both literally as part of the huge boom in those going on physical pilgrimages which has been one of the most significant spiritual developments over the last 25 years, but also in terms of outlook and attitude. Surveys show that a majority of contemporary Christians describe their faith as an ongoing journey rather than a once-and-for-all conversion. This represents a significant change of attitude over the last 50 years. Whereas in the 1960s around two-thirds of Christians talked of a single conversion experience and one-third of an ongoing journey of faith, these proportions are now reversed in poll findings. The road to Emmaus, with its story of gradual realization and walking alongside one another, is a more potent metaphor of faith for many now than the road to Damascus with its sudden blinding moment of conversion. This is a great source of hope for the reclamation of open liberal theology with its invitation to a perpetual pilgrimage of walking in faith rather than certainty and travelling hopefully rather than being sure that one has arrived and is right about everything.

What does it mean to be a pilgrim church? First and foremost, being open, both literally and metaphorically. A pilgrim church is an unlocked church, open through the week so that people can wander in and be turned from tourists into pilgrims. Its worship has room for mystery, embraces the numinous and includes times of quiet for openness to the Spirit. It is theologically open, accommodating those who are seekers and explorers on the fringes of faith. There is an increasing need for mooring-places where people can linger awhile, as well as harbours where they can drop anchor and remain. Some churches provide a welcoming place to come home to, as the father did for the prodigal son. Others, however, are more like filling-stations where people can pull in, pause awhile and fill up with spiritual sustenance before continuing on their journey. Pilgrim churches, like pilgrim people, are on the move. They are not static but rather on a journey and looking forward as well as back. Like the people of Israel as they wandered through the wilderness on the way to the promised land, they are conscious that God is also on the move and ahead of them. Jean Vanier, the visionary founder of the *L'Arche* communities, observed: 'A sect has control at its heart, a community has journey at its heart.' In similar vein, William Sloane Coffin maintained that 'we can build a community out of seekers of truth but not out of possessors of truth'.[35]

Open pilgrim churches offer hope rather than dogmatic certainty. They are fuzzy at the edges. Fuzziness is, indeed, one of the cardinal liberal virtues. Infuriating dogmatists and fundamentalists and confirming them in their view that liberals stand for nothing and fall for anything, it is, in fact, not an easy opting out of difficult and uncomfortable decisions but a manifestation of that responsibility, modesty and openness that Barth identified at the heart of truly liberal faith. In a recent apologia for liberal Anglicanism, Jonathan Clatworthy proposes a set of characteristics similar to those I have set out above for churches adopting what he calls a coherentist approach. They are 'undogmatic, developing, critical, public, engaged and comfortable with fuzzy edges'. They do not expect true belief in all members but rather prefer to hear a wide variety of voices. They accord an important role to scholarship and they are willing to change.[36] Alongside these open pilgrim churches, we need a new breed of priests and pastors who walk alongside their congregations as fellow pilgrims as well as watching over them as shepherds. John Killinger captures something of what is required in this description of the kind of minister that people believe in:

Somebody who is clearly struggling with life and its issues and bothers to phrase his discoveries, or even his questions, in such a way as to speak to their own conscious and unconscious concerns

about the same things . . . a sensitive, creative, poetic figure, grap-
pling with the problems of being human and secular and whole in
our time, and sharing both the quest and the results with other
individuals . . . this is finally the only justification for being paid a
salary to be a minister . . . to be their freed man . . . their freed
mind, their freed heart, their freed conscience, their freed dreamer,
their freed critic, their freed believer.[37]

The fifth and final area where a greater sense of openness is badly
needed by believers today is in our openness to others and readiness to
concede that we all have only partial truths. This means being more
tentative and humble in our own beliefs. Fundamentalists will scoff that
the liberal trumpet is yet again giving an uncertain sound, but there is in
fact a clarity and even a boldness in this position. Robert Runcie articulated it well in his enthronement sermon as Archbishop of Canterbury
in 1980: 'The cry is "The Church must give a firm lead". Yes. It must –
a firm lead against rigid thinking, a judging temper of mind, the disposition to oversimplify difficult and complex problems. If the Church
gives Jesus Christ's sort of lead, it will not be popular.'[38] Having an
open liberal theology means being prepared to change one's mind, to
admit one has been mistaken and to display something of the vulnerability that characterized Jesus and the 'total personal modesty' extolled
by Barth. It is perhaps the special vocation of Christians, who are called
to turn the other cheek and walk the extra mile, but the quality of being
open to the insights and teachings of other traditions is valued in most
religions. Reflecting on the observation of the Jewish sages: 'Who is
wise? One who learns from all men', Jonathan Sacks writes: 'The wisest
is not one who knows himself wiser than others: he is one who knows
all men have some share of the truth and is willing to learn from them,
for none of us knows all the truth and each of us knows some of it.'[39]
Christians Aware, a wonderfully open and inclusive group that seeks
to spread understanding of different faiths and traditions, has as its
guiding principle the words of Ronald Wynne, 'Do not try to teach
anyone anything until you have learned something from them.'
A key element of this is openness to the truth found in other religions. This has long been a characteristic of liberal theology. In Donald
Miller's words, 'Liberals are open to the truth of other religions. Chris-

tianity is not viewed as the only expression of man's search for God or of God's revelation to man.'[40] Such openness has become particularly important when globalization, large-scale immigration and the internet have brought us all much closer together and where different faiths, cultures and perspectives co-exist cheek by jowl. Whereas in the past it was possible for you to be in your small corner and I in mine, nowadays we are thrown together willy-nilly. Unfortunately this closer proximity to the other has all too often bred fear, prejudice and suspicion, especially in faith communities.

There is, in fact, no good reason why globalization, immigration and the spread of the internet should not bring about more openness, respect, hospitality and enthusiastic engagement with the traditions and insights of others. An open theological attitude does not mean evacuating and hollowing out one's own beliefs. This is where the balance provided by order comes in. Without some sense of being at ease with oneself and one's own position, it is impossible to be truly open to others. Openness is rooted in stability and order. Advocating the virtues of a 'hospitable establishment' in terms of the Church of England's attitude to other faiths, another recent Archbishop of Canterbury, George Carey, pointed out that 'in order to be hospitable to others, one first needs a home'.[41] Even more important than the link with order, however, is the relationship between openness and grace. We are open to others in response to that gracious and generous outpouring of God's love and to the openness of the Spirit of truth and love, 'bearing the lamp of grace' in the words of the hymn, 'Thou, Whose Almighty Word'. Another of Andrew Pratt's hymns provides an appropriate bridge between this chapter and the next and does so by taking us back to the Holy Spirit flying wild and free:

> We come by many different paths,
> Each certain that our way is true.
> As sisters, brothers, let us talk,
> A way to peace is overdue.
> Caged in a creed, we think we've caught
> The source of all that is to be,
> But God cannot be thus confined:
> The Spirit's flying, wild and free!

We think that we alone have found
The secret goal of all the earth;
We make our rules, oppress the weak,
With shackles hold them from their birth.
Within four walls we idolise
The treasures of our certainty.
We worship all that we have made.
Outside God sits in poverty.

So, prophets of this present age
Disturb us in our arrogance
To let the Spirit freely blow,
To offer love's extravagance.
For love can shake our self-conceit,
Tear up each creed, each guarantee;
Confronting cant and human pride,
God demonstrates love's quality.[42]

Notes

1. J. Moltmann, *Theology of Hope* (London: SCM Press, 1967); W. H. Vanstone, *The Stature of Waiting* (London: Darton, Longman & Todd, 1982); Bradley 2000, Chapter 6; Bradley 2009.
2. K. Ward, *Religion and Revelation* (Oxford: Oxford University Press, 1994), pp. 339–40.
3. Hick and Knitter 1988, p. 109.
4. Cauthen 1983, p. 24.
5. E-mail, 3 November 2008.
6. 'The Bright Wind is Blowing' by Cecily Taylor. Reproduced by permission of Stainer & Bell Ltd, 23 Gruneisen Road, London N3 1DZ, www.stainer.co.uk.
7. On the original meaning of *Yasha* and its subsequent distortion, see P. Webb, *Salvation Today* (London: SCM Press, 1974) and P. Potter, *Life In All Its Fullness* (Geneva: World Council of Churches, 1981).
8. D. Hilton, *My Testimony: The Origins of a Liberal Faith* (*Free to Believe* pamphlet, n.d.) pp. 17–18.
9. 'A Progressive View', *Life and Work*, September 2008, p. 13.
10. *Congregational Praise* (London: Independent Press, 1951) No. 230. See also George Caird's 'Not Far Beyond the Sea' in *Rejoice and Sing* (Oxford: Oxford University Press, 1991), No. 318.

11. 'Face to Faith', *Guardian*, 12 July 2008.
12. *Life And Work*, September 2008, p. 13.
13. E. Schillebeeckx, *Church: The Human Story of God* (London: SCM Press, 1990), p. 167.
14. Quoted in M. Camroux, *Coming Out as a Liberal* (*Free to Believe* pamphlet, n.d.), p. 2.
15. Sacks 2002, p. 65.
16. Clatworthy 2008, p. 219.
17. Hilton, *My Testimony*, p. 21.
18. *Ibid.*, pp. 2–3.
19. C. A. Patrides (ed.), *Complete English Poems of John Donne* (London: Dent, 1985), p. 228.
20. *The Cloud of Unknowing* (Harmondsworth: Penguin, 1961), p. 59.
21. G. MacLeod, *The Whole Earth Shall Cry Glory* (Glasgow: Wild Goose Publications, 2007), p. 24.
22. Camroux, *Coming Out as a Liberal*, p. 2.
23. Quoted in Cauthen 1983, p. viii.
24. Hilton, *My Testimony*, p. 11.
25. 'Praise the Source of Faith and Learning' by Thomas Troeger, © Oxford University Press Inc. 1986. Reproduced by permission of Oxford University Press. All rights reserved.
26. Kurzman 1998, pp. 255–69.
27. 'The Allure of the Open Future', *Guardian*, 29 August 1988.
28. James Gregory lecture, St Andrew's University, 9 October 2008.
29. Pratt 2002, p. 81. Reproduced by permission of Stainer & Bell Ltd, 23 Gruneisen Road, London N3 1DZ, www.stainer.co.uk.
30. 'Hope Through the Scriptures' in Alker 2008, pp. 31, 35.
31. 'The Permafrost and the African Bible – Second Reflections on the Lambeth Conference' (internet post, 2008).
32. Scottish Interfaith Day, St Andrew's, 30 November 2008.
33. Killinger 1971, pp. 184–5.
34. Bradley 1992, p. 62.
35. For a fuller discussion on the marks of a pilgrim church and people, see Bradley 2009, pp. 83–5.
36. Clatworthy 2008, p. 231.
37. Killinger 1971, pp. 156–7.
38. Bradley 1992, p. 220.
39. Sacks 2002, p. 65.
40. 'Liberalism' in A. Richardson and J. Bowden, *A New Dictionary of Christian Theology* (London: SCM Press, 1983), p. 324.
41. 'Holding Together: Church and Nation in the 21st Century', lecture delivered on 23 April 2002, p. 9.
42. Pratt 2002, p. 96. Reproduced by permission of Stainer & Bell Ltd, 23 Gruneisen Road, London N3 1DZ, www.stainer.co.uk.

6

Diversity

Diversity and pluralism have always appealed to the liberal mind. J. S. Mill's classic work *On Liberty* is a tirade against social conformity and argues that diversity is a key measure and element of human well-being. 'Different persons require different conditions for their spiritual development,' he wrote, 'and without a diversity in their modes of life they do not grow up to the mental, moral and aesthetic stature of which their natures are capable.'[1] Liberal theology similarly values diversity and difference. Thanks in considerable part to the effects of globalization and large-scale migration, cultural, ethnic, religious and political diversity is an increasingly dominant characteristic of our contemporary world and is directly affecting the lives of many people in a way that was often not the case for previous generations. The effects of climate change and environmental degradation have at the same time made us acutely aware of the importance of biodiversity. Greater exposure to pluralism and diversity can push us in one of two ways – either towards fear and fundamentalism or into a realization of what Jonathan Sacks calls the dignity of difference. This chapter will argue that the scriptures and sacred texts of all the major world faiths share the conviction that the diversity which characterizes the world represents the will and intention of the creator. It will further argue that for Christians at least, diversity is also a key characteristic of God.

If, as I have suggested in the three previous chapters, grace, order and openness can be seen as the key attributes of the three persons of the Christian Godhead, then it is surely even more the case that diversity is an essential and defining attribute of God conceived as Trinity – three in one and one in three. The Christian doctrine of the Trinity proclaims that God is not a single monochrome self-sufficient entity but rather a community of persons in relationship with each other. God is not uni-dimensional: relationality, mutuality and diversity are at the very heart and core of the Godhead. The doctrine of the Trinity moves the emphasis from a God who commands to a God who relates. There is a deep if seemingly paradoxical link here between unity and diversity. The unity of God is created in and through irreducible diversity. The divine persons of the Trinity form their unity through diversity. Theologians have struggled to describe this seeming paradox. Perhaps it is best left to poets like the unknown author of 'St Patrick's Breastplate' which brings together grace, order and diversity in its evocation of the Trinitarian God:

> For my shield this day I call
> A mighty power:
> The Holy Trinity!
> Affirming threeness,
> Confessing oneness,
> In the making of all
> Through love.[2]

For liberal theologians the Trinity is the starting point for an open pluralistic theology that embraces the other. Raimundo Panikkar, who sees it as the ultimate and perpetually generative source, from which rises form and determination and which is constantly realized in the flux of active life, has written that 'the mystery of the Trinity is the ultimate foundation of pluralism'.[3] Marjorie Suchochi writes that 'for the human to be made in the image of God is for the human to exist in community that is itself created in and through irreducible diversity'.[4] Leonardo Boff expounds the idea of the social Trinity, particularly popular with liberation theologians, calling people to revel in and respect diversity and writing that 'seeing people as the image and likeness of the Trinity implies always seeing them in open relationship with others; it is only through being with others, understanding themselves as others see them, that they can build up their own identities'.[5] Mary Grey represents a view common among feminist theologians in seeking to define human personality in terms of relation rather than achievement:

God as Trinity expresses not only the mutuality of relation between persons, but their distinctiveness, diversity, *otherness* and the need to respect this. That the other can be transformed from the threatening *other* to the beloved *other* is a concern at the heart of feminist theology.[6]

Central to the Christian doctrine of the Trinity is the concept of perichoresis or mutual exchange. It holds that the three persons of the Trinity, while each maintaining their own identity and distinctiveness, interpenetrate and overlap each other. Jürgen Moltmann has made much of the importance of this idea in his own faith journey from a God of domination and obedience to a God of network and community. For him, perichoresis is about personhood without individualism, movement from one to another, embrace and encompassing.

In the Trinity there is simultaneously complete movement and absolute rest, as in the eye of the hurricane. The Trinity is not closed like a circle or a triangle but wide open. The whole created world can find within it rest, freedom, life, space and a home. It is an inviting environment open by virtue of the graciously overflowing love which is at its centre. We are not swallowed up in a divine ocean but we find ourselves in a wide space where there is a room of one's own.[7]

Perichoresis is perhaps best conceived as a dance of divine love which flows in constant motion from and through one to the other of the three persons of the Godhead and out beyond them through the world. The idea is well expressed in the prayer of dismissal in the liturgy used in Iona Abbey: 'May our life in community reflect the dance of the Trinity by which the world is blessed.'

It is only fair to acknowledge that it is not just liberals who are attracted to this theme. The late Colin Gunton is one of a number of conservative theologians who have made much of the idea of perichoresis. His book, *The One, the Three, the Many*, argues that God's being and God's world have been over-associated with unity in Western thought and need to be seen rather in terms of both unity and plurality: 'Trinitarian conceptuality enables us to think of our world as both, and in different respects, one and many, but also one and many in relation.'[8] On the whole, however, in thinking about God, conservative theologians tend to emphasize unity and exclusiveness, and liberals diversity and open plurality.

In terms of its understanding of God, Trinitarian Christianity stands between the polytheism of Eastern religions and the radical exclusive monotheism of Judaism and Islam. Hinduism has perhaps the fullest conception of divine diversity with its worship of a multiplicity of gods. It is surely no coincidence that one of the outstanding pioneer exponents of religious pluralism in the early twentieth century was the Hindu philosopher, Sarvapelli Radhakrishnan (1888–1975). At the other extreme, Judaism, and to a much greater extent Islam, emphasize the oneness of God. 'I am the Lord your God', the Lord tells Moses when issuing the Ten Commandments, 'You shall have no other Gods but me' (Deuteronomy 5.7). Moses is later told: 'Hear, O Israel: The Lord our God is one Lord' (Deuteronomy 6.4). Islam has an even more emphatic sense of God's exclusive oneness. Allah has no partner and does not consist of different elements or parts. For Muslims, it is wrong to see humans as being created in God's image, and a blasphemous impossibility to think in terms of God having a son. Jesus is an honoured prophet, no more and no less. For Muslims and Jews the Trinitarian perspective of Christianity which lets God be seen as a being in community and the attendant concept of perichoresis is largely lacking.

But if there are substantial differences between the world's major faiths about the extent to which diversity is found within the heart of the Godhead, there is a clear agreement in their sacred texts that God deliberately created a world teeming with difference and that God revels in this diversity. On this point the Hebrew Bible and the Koran concur with the Christian New Testament, the Upanishads and the *Rig Veda*. They are also agreed in distinguishing two key aspects of this divinely ordained diversity in the world: the rich differentiation of living species which we now call biodiversity; and the cultural, ethnic, linguistic and religious diversity found among humans.

The clearest and most important affirmation of biodiversity as God's express intention and delight is found in the pages of the Hebrew Bible. This is evident from the opening chapter of Genesis where God is portrayed as creating heaven, earth, seas, plants of every kind and 'swarms of living creatures' filling the seas, the skies and the land. Three things stand out in this account – the emphasis on diversity expressed in the repeated phrase 'according to their kinds' used about different categories of living creature; the intrinsic goodness of creation, underlined by the statement at the end of every stage of creation that God 'saw that it was good'; and the lack of anthropocentrism, with humans being a very important part of the story but not the centre of it. The overriding sense conveyed in the Genesis 1 story of creation is of a world teeming with diversity, richness and variety. It is the message conveyed in that very simple and very biblical hymn,

> All things bright and beautiful,
> all creatures great and small,
> all things wise and wonderful,
> the Lord God made them all.

The emphasis on diversity is maintained in the story of the flood where Noah is commanded to take with him in the ark two of every kind of living creature and in the covenant that God makes after the flood not just with all humanity but with all living things. It is reinforced with particular power in the Psalms which point to the pleroma or fullness of God's creation in such verses as 'The earth is the Lord's and the fullness thereof' (Psalm 24.1) and proclaim that every part of creation has a significance and importance to God in its own right – not just for its usefulness to humans:

> The trees of the Lord are watered abundantly,
> The cedars of Lebanon which he planted.
> In them the birds build their nests;
> The stork has her home in the fir trees.
> The high mountains are for the wild goat;
> The rocks are a refuge for the badgers.
>
> (Psalm 104.16–18)

This theme is repeated in the reminder given to Job that God's work includes bringing rain on the desert where no man is (Job 38.26).

There is a delicate balance and a progression between the universal and the particular in the way in which the Hebrew Bible describes God's creation of the natural physical world and relationship with it. Initially the emphasis is on wide universal categories such as water, earth, light, darkness, vegetation and living creatures, although even in the opening chapter of Genesis there is already a sense of differentiation into species and kinds. Later, however, the Hebrew Bible moves from the universal to the particular in its treatment of God's relationship with the created world. This shift is very clear in the Psalms with the specificity of references to individual species such as the wild goat, badgers and cedars of Lebanon mentioned above. Jesus also moves from the universal to the particular in the way in which he focuses in his teaching on such specific examples as the lily of the field and the sparrows sold for a penny.

This progression from the universal to the particular in the biblical account of creation and God's continuing dealings with the natural world mirrors the progression from simplicity to complexity that lies at the heart of the evolutionary process. It portrays God's purpose and activity to be wholly consistent with what the theory of evolution demonstrates, namely the progressive development of a world of ever greater complexity and diversity, where the simple molecule eventually develops into the human brain with its millions of neuro-transmitters. All theistic faiths agree in seeing a progression from simplicity to complexity, and from chaos to form and beauty, as a central aspect of the ordered nature of creation. This brings us back to the key attribute of order highlighted in Chapter 4. It also accords with the emphasis of the relatively new field of complexity theory which is engaging many contemporary scientists and marks a significant shift in scientific priorities from splitting and dividing to studying how systems behave in their complexity.

Although the emphasis in the Hebrew Bible switches progressively from the universal to the particular, it does not portray a world made up of a collection of autonomous, independent individual entities. Rather, it suggests a rich and varied creation united in interdependence and mutuality. Creation is portrayed as being especially brought together in praising its maker with whom there is a wonderful reciprocal relationship. The Psalms and the prophetic books are both full of images of diverse creatures responding to the lure and love of their creator, with birds and animals lifting their voices in song, rivers and streams gurgling their joy, the trees of the field clapping their hands, and mountains and hills skipping forth like goats. This symphony of praise finds its fullest expression in the song of the three young men in Daniel 3.26–30 and is, of course, the subject of Francis of Assisi's great Canticle of the Creatures.

These images convey a very important theological message which is crucial to understanding the theological significance of diversity, its importance to God, the reason for its existence and its delicate interplay with unity. It was classically expounded by Thomas Aquinas in his reflection on the Genesis story of creation in which he linked diversity with God's goodness and grace.

> Distinction and variety in the world is intended by the first cause. God brings things into existence in order that his goodness may be communicated and manifested. One solitary creature would not suffice. Therefore he makes creatures many and diverse, that what is wanting in one may be supplied by another. Goodness in God is single and consistent, in creatures scattered and uneven; hence the whole universe together participates in the divine goodness more perfectly and represents it better than any single creature whatever. Things are made distinct by the concept of wisdom.[9]

This has profound implications for the way in which we think about and treat the non-human part of creation. Once we really grasp this idea of the pleroma or fullness of God's creation and the significance of every part of it, then we can surely no longer go on destroying whales, cutting down tropical rain forests or turning the good earth into dust bowls and deserts.[10]

Turning from the biological to the cultural, ethnic, linguistic and religious spheres, the Hebrew Bible also makes clear that diversity is God's purpose and desire, although there is rather more ambiguity and tension in this area between the universal and particular and between unity and diversity. The key foundational text here is the story of the tower of Babel in which God scatters people across the earth and gives them different languages in response to the action of humans in building a tower to reach the heavens (Genesis 11.1–9). This story, which is clearly designed to provide an explanation for why there are different languages and why the human population is spread out across the globe, has long been taken as indicating that cultural and linguistic diversity was not, in fact, God's original intention but rather an after-thought representing a departure from God's preferred plan for unity and uniformity. In this reading, God's action at Babel in scattering people across the earth and deliberately confusing their language was seen as an angry punishment imposed on erring and recalcitrant humanity. It seemed to show God's strident ethnocentricy and pes-simistic view of cultural pluralism and has reinforced attitudes of exclu-sivism and monoculturalism. In the words of Madeleine Bunting, 'Babel became a trope for all western cultures' most profound pes-simism about possibilities of diversity and the freedoms of the city.'[11]

Significant recent work by both Jewish and Christian scholars has substantially reinterpreted the message of this story. A good example is to be found in Jonathan Sacks' prophetic book *The Dignity of Differ-ence*. He points out that the people on the plain at Shinar who form the centrepiece of the story are seeking both uniformity and Godlike power. Their intention is to create a man-made environment – the city with its tower reaching up to the heavens – that will replicate the structure of the cosmos, but where humans will rule, not God. For Sacks, this represents an attempt to impose man-made unity on divinely created diversity. God's actions at Babel establish diversity or difference at the heart of human life. The division of humankind into a multiplicity of different languages, cultures, nations and civilizations is motivated by a desire to teach the importance of difference and the worth of the other in the face of human arrogance and pride. It marks a crucial turning-point in the biblical narrative from the universal to the particular in respect of culture, ethnicity and language, paralleling the similar pro-gression we have noted in respect of the world of nature and biological evolution. It is important that the universal comes first and that God's covenant with Noah is with all humankind, and indeed all living things. When God moves on from this universal covenant to establish a partic-ular relationship with the people of Israel, it is not in an exclusivist spirit but rather to reinforce the importance of diversity.

God, the creator of humanity, having made a covenant with all humanity, then turns to one people and commands it to be different in order to teach humanity the dignity of difference. Biblical monotheism is not the idea that there is one God and therefore one truth, one faith, one way of life. On the contrary, it is the idea that unity creates diversity.[12]

More radically, Theodore Hiebert has recently argued through careful linguistic analysis that the Babel story shows cultural and linguistic diversity to be God's design for the world rather than a punishment for it. The theme of the story is that, if left to itself, the human race would preserve a uniform culture and a single language. God intervenes to diversify culture first by multiplying languages, so creating a polyglot world, and then by dispersing the human population. There is no element of punishment involved, rather 'God's introduction of cultural difference through linguistic and geographical diversity is presented as God's intention for the world'. Far from having a pessimistic message about cultural and ethnic pluralism, the story of Babel in fact presents an optimistic view of it as divinely inspired and ordained.[13]

The story of the tower of Babel is immediately followed in the Hebrew Bible by the appearance of Abraham, whose name in Hebrew means 'father of multitudes' and who is acknowledged as biological and spiritual ancestor by Jews, Christians and Muslims today. Abraham himself is not a Jew, a Christian or a Muslim – he epitomizes both unity and diversity, pre-dating the separation of humanity into distinct ethnic and religious identities and straddling the move from the universal to the particular which comes with the divine decision to relate with humanity through one chosen people. As in the realm of nature, so in the realm of cultural, religious and ethnic identity, the Hebrew Bible describes a progression from the universal to the particular. This is most graphically illustrated by the identity of the partners with whom God successively enters into covenant – first with all humanity after the flood (Genesis 9.1–17), then with a particular family through Abraham (Genesis 17.1–27), and thirdly and finally with a particular people in the covenant with Israel on Mount Sinai (Exodus 31.12–18). There is undoubtedly a tension in the Hebrew Bible between the themes of universality and particularism, represented in the ethnocentricity displayed in the divine choice of the people of Israel. There is also a sense of purposeful progression from the one to the other motivated by God's preference for diversity. Indeed, it is diversity that links the universal with the particular and provides a bridge between them. In the words of Sacks: 'Universality – the covenant with Noah – is only the context and prelude to the irreducible multiplicity of cultures, those systems of meaning by which human beings have sought to understand their relationships to one another, the world and the source of being.'[14] He goes on:

> The God of Abraham teaches humanity a more complex truth than simple oppositions – particular/universal, individual/state, tribe/humanity – would allow. We are particular *and* universal, the same *and* different, human beings as such, but also members of this family, that community, this history, that heritage. Our particularity is our window on to universality, just as our language is the only way we have of understanding the world we share with speakers of other languages. God no more wants all faiths and cultures to be the same than a loving parent wants his or her children to be the same. That is the conceptual link between love, creation and difference. We serve God, author of diversity, by respecting diversity.[15]

The exegesis by Sacks and others of the stories of Babel and Abraham is extremely important in countering the exclusivity and ethnocentrism which can so easily be read into the Hebrew Bible's account of the divine election of a particular people. There are other themes and stories within it which point to God's ongoing relationship with those beyond the chosen people of Israel. Particularly important is the way in which what have been called 'the pagan saints of the Old Testament' are incorporated into God's covenant. These are of two kinds: those like Abel, Enoch and Noah who precede God's covenants with Abraham and Moses; and those like Job, Melchizedek, Lot and the Queen of Sheba who are contemporary with the Israelite dispensation but outside it because they are non-Jews and come from other nations. Two of the Bible's most heroic women, Tamar and Ruth, are not Israelites. The first is a Canaanite, the second a Moabite, yet each has a place of honour in Israel's history, and both are ancestors of its greatest king, David. The Hebrew Bible witnesses repeatedly to the holiness of these 'pagan saints', who are often described as 'walking with God', and is clear about their inclusion in God's covenant. For the great French scholar of religion, Jean Danielou, they are the prototypes of the salvation of pagans and the prophets of cosmic religion who demonstrate that God is concerned with all humanity in its diversity and not just a chosen portion.[16]

Another key theme in the Hebrew Bible is that of the stranger in our midst. It is striking that whereas in the whole of the Pentateuch there is just one reference to loving your neighbour as yourself, the command to 'love the stranger' occurs no fewer than 36 times. A typical example is in Leviticus 19.34: 'The stranger who sojourns with you shall be to you as the native among you, and you shall love him as yourself; for you were strangers in the land of Egypt.' The inescapable emphasis here is on the imperative of reaching out towards and embracing the other.

Perhaps the most striking testimony to the value of religious diversity and pluralism in the Hebrew Bible is contained in that great passage which looks forward to a peaceable kingdom where men will hammer their swords into ploughshares and their spears into pruning hooks (Micah 4.1–5). Micah ends his inspiring vision of the peaceable kingdom with the words that 'all peoples will go forward, each in the name of its gods, while we go forward in the name of Yahweh our God'. The prophet envisages the nations of the world streaming to Mount Zion in order to learn the ways of God. As a result of their encounter with Yahweh, they will learn the ways of peace and harmony, how to love and embrace the stranger and the other, but they will not give up their diversity or their own beliefs. Rather, they will continue to follow their own religions just as the Jews remain committed to their beliefs. Religious and cultural diversity rather than unity is the hallmark of the ideal peaceable society realized by following God's ways as envisioned by the prophet.

The Jewish tradition is not alone in suggesting the God-given nature of human diversity. It is a recurrent theme in the sacred scriptures of Islam, as these extracts from the Koran show:

Men, we have created you from a male and female and divided you
into nations and tribes that you might get to know one another.
(Sura 49.13)

Among Allah's other signs are the creation of heaven and earth and
the diversity of your tongues and colours. Surely there are signs in
this for all mankind. (Sura 30.22)

We have ordained a law and assigned a path for each of you. Had
Allah pleased, He could have made you one nation: but it is His
wish to prove you by that which He has bestowed upon you. Vie
with each other in good works, for to Allah you shall all return and
He will declare to you what you have disagreed about. (Sura 5.48)

The message of these and other passages in the Koran is, as the contemporary French Muslim scholar, Bruno Guiderdoni, says, that 'God
praises and loves diversity'.[17] They also introduce the interesting idea
that God has created different cultures and peoples so that they might
'vie with each other in good works'. Perhaps there is an echo here of
Aquinas' explanation for the variety of creation and a sense that no one
people can adequately reflect the breadth and variety of God's goodness
and grace. Like the Hebrew Bible, the Koran balances unity and diversity. For all its teaching that diversity and pluralism is God-given, there
is also a strong emphasis that everything has its source in the one God
and that all shall return to that single source.

This last theme is also very evident in the Christian New Testament
with its portrayal of Jesus Christ as the one in whom all things cohere
and will be gathered together. As in the Hebrew Bible and the Koran,
there is a certain tension and ambiguity in the New Testament between
unity and diversity, the universal and the particular. It is focused on the
person and teaching of Jesus. Is he an advocate of unity over diversity,
as several of his sayings would suggest, and even more a symbol of particularism and exclusiveness, as he is so often taken to be both by some
of his most ardent followers and by his foes, or does Jesus rather both
demonstrate and teach the value of diversity and difference, and
practise and preach radical inclusiveness?

The well-known statement, 'I am the way, and the truth, and the life;

no one comes to the Father, but by me' (John 14.6) does not seem to offer much room for religious diversity or pluralism and it is hardly surprising that it has been taken as a proof text for Christian uniqueness and exclusivity. As I have already noted, however, this self-description does not necessarily carry a closed, narrow, exclusive meaning, certainly not if it is taken in conjunction with the way that Jesus is portrayed in the Gospels as the one who deliberately goes out of his comfort zone and reaches beyond his natural kith and kin to establish relationships with those radically different from himself, ethnically and culturally, and often seen as beyond the pale (see pages 106–8). From their opening nativity narratives populated with shepherds, angels and wise men, through their descriptions of the motley crew that made up his disciples and of the unusually prominent role played by women in the context of a life lived in first-century Palestine, to their continual emphasis on his own preference for encounter and interaction with the stranger and the other, the Gospels present diversity as perhaps the most striking and consistent theme in Jesus' life.

The apparent exclusivity of John 14.6 is balanced by other statements attributed to Jesus suggesting a preference for diversity and pluralism. In the same Gospel he talks of his father's house having many mansions (John 14.2) and remarks that 'there are other sheep of mine, not belonging to this fold' (John 10.16) with its implication that his mission and his concern are not limited and restricted to a particular group or people. His admiration for the faith of the Roman centurion leads him to reflect that 'people will come from east and west and sit at table with Abraham, Isaac, and Jacob in the kingdom of heaven, while the sons of the kingdom will be thrown into the outer darkness' (Matthew 8.11–12). That remark echoes a common theme of Jesus, that narrow, judgemental religious bigots are often furthest from the kingdom of God, while those seen as outsiders and outcasts are often closest to it.

Unity is also a major theme of Jesus' sayings as recorded in John's Gospel. He prays to God that those who follow and believe in him 'may all be one, as you Father are in me, and I in you' and that 'they may become perfectly one' (John 17.20, 23). The New Testament as a whole makes much of the unity that is to be found in and through Jesus Christ and portrays him as the one who brings all things together. This idea is expressed particularly forcefully and eloquently by Paul who prophesies that 'in the dispensation of the fullness of times God might gather together in one all things in Christ' and writes of 'the fullness of him who fills all in all' (Ephesians 1.10, 23). This language suggests an inclusive broadness and ample plenitude about the unity which Christ embodies rather than a narrow exclusivity. Indeed, these texts have resonated with and inspired theological liberals, especially in the golden age of the late nineteenth century. T. H. Green declared: 'The glory of Christianity is not that it excludes, but that it comprehends . . . that it is the expression of a common spirit, which is gathering together all things in one.'[18] George Matheson saw Christianity as embracing and incorporating all previous faiths. Far from crushing or annihilating them, it 'has made them vivid by making them living' and provided 'a point in which beliefs hitherto deemed at variance may lie down together in unity':

> In its many-sidedness it has a side for each of these [other religions]. It has let in its light upon them; it has given its breath to them; it has found a place for them in its own system. It has given them a logical order . . . In the comprehensive temple of Christian truth there is not only a niche which each may fill, but a niche which, at some stage of its development, must be filled by one and all.[19]

Characteristically, Matheson expressed his view in a poem, at the head of which he quoted Ephesians 1.10:

> Gather us in, Thou Love that fillest all;
> Gather our rival faiths within Thy fold;
> Rend each man's temple veil, and bid it fall,
> That we may know that Thou hast been of old.
>
> Gather us in – we worship only Thee;
> In varied names we stretch a common hand;
> In diverse forms a common soul we see;
> In many ships we seek one spirit land.

Each sees one colour of Thy rainbow-light,
Each looks upon one tint and calls it heaven;
Thou art the fullness of our partial sight;
We are not perfect till we find the seven.

Some seek a Father in the heav'ns above;
Some ask a human image to adore;
Some crave a spirit vast as life and love;
Within Thy mansions we have all and more.[20]

This is a classic expression of what has come to be known as the inclusivist position in terms of Christian attitudes towards other faiths. It holds that Christ as Logos or Universal Love embraces all faiths and is to be found in them, even when he is not explicitly acknowledged or identified. We have already encountered other expressions of inclusivism in the Logos theology of Justin Martyr and Karl Rahner's concept of anonymous Christianity (see pages 86 & 58). For some liberals it remains too imperialistic and condescending, just as for most conservatives it is not exclusive enough. For many liberal Christians, however, the sentiments of Matheson's 'Gather Us In' will strike a deep chord, not least its reminder that each of us has only a partial view and sees just one colour of God's rainbow light. The whole poem is pervaded by a wonderfully liberal sense of the wideness of God's grace, the love that fills all and embraces diversity, gathers us in and rends the walls that we erect to protect our own individual temples.

The emphasis that Matheson, following Paul, puts on Christ gathering all in serves as an important reminder that the liberal Christian embrace of diversity does not mean an attachment to dualism. Diversity is balanced by unity, just as freedom is by order. There is no room in liberal theology for a dualistic division between matter and spirit. It is strongly monist, holding to the doctrine that there is one supreme being, as opposed to a good and an evil principle existing as rival powers. In emphasizing the value of diversity, the liberal theological tradition does not deny the fundamental oneness of the world, the inter-connectedness of all things and the idea that God is present and can be discovered and known in all things. It affirms with the Hebridean crofter:

There is no plant in the ground
But is full of His virtue,
There is no form in the strand
But is full of His blessing.[21]

In Christianity, as within other faiths, there is a delicate and complex symbiotic relationship between unity and diversity. I am not sure that we always get the balance right in our expression of that relationship in our liturgies or in our actions. An example that springs to mind is found in the opening responses of the morning service in the Iona Abbey Worship Book which include the phrase: 'How good it is, how wonderful, to live together in unity.' I have to say that I find it impossible to say the second half of this affirmation which is a congregational response. This is partly because I feel it is simply untrue – we do not live together in unity whether as Christians, as members of different faiths or simply as members of the human race – but nor am I at all sure that it is what we are called by God to do. As those who have sat around me during morning worship in Iona Abbey will testify, I find myself impelled to say *sotto voce*: 'How good it is, how wonderful, to live together in diversity.' My own understanding of the scriptural passages quoted above, and indeed of the whole drift of both the Hebrew Bible and the New Testament, leads me to believe that this is what God requires and wants of us.

Another area where Christians, and not least liberal Christians, have perhaps been insufficiently open to the benefit of divinely inspired diversity, is in the pursuit of church unity. Throughout much of the twentieth century, liberals were in the vanguard of efforts to reunite the divided denominations of Protestant Christianity in a single church. I am not at all sure that we are now called to that task, if indeed we ever were. Christians are most certainly called to work together, to reach out to, understand and learn from each other, but I question whether we are called to work for the elimination of different denominations and traditions and to erode the wide diversity that exists within the Church. If one considers the diversity within scripture, the considerable differences that existed in the early Church, the way Paul dealt separately and distinctly with the various Christian communities to whom he wrote his letters, and the constant dividing and sub-dividing of churches throughout Christian history, one has to ask whether Christian unity is, in fact, an essential expression of God's unfolding purpose. The liberal-led movement for church unity found itself frustrated and running into the sand partly because it did not respect diversity and difference enough, as Rob Wheway of the Liberal Institute has pointed out:

> In the 1960s when Christian unity started, the aim was to have the different denominations integrated into one church. It soon became apparent that worshippers valued their own specific beliefs and methods of worship. While they welcomed the dialogue and worshipping together, they would not relinquish their own faith and practices – or cultures. So multiculturalism, not integration, became the way to unity.
>
> This respect for each other's way of doing things meant that the other person's faith was valued because it gave different insights; it recognised that we are all struggling to discover the truth in different ways.[22]

In recent years, what I and others have characterized as the 'ecumaniac' outlook which prevailed for most of the second half of the twentieth century and which sought to achieve ecclesial union through institutional means has given way to a more grassroots and *ad hoc* approach where diversity and difference are respected. Local collaborative initiatives flourish but large-scale institutional church union is now off the agenda. The 'ecumaniac' view that passionately held differences could be ended by reports couched in sufficiently bland terms has given way to a pilgrim spirit which recognizes the value of treading the road together, sharing, learning and maybe even resting on one another's shoulders for a while, but accepting that in the end people may diverge to take different routes to the promised land.[23] The growth of this pilgrim spirit, and its application to inter-faith as well as inter-church relations, is a welcome expression of confidence in the openness of the liberal theological tradition.

If this changing approach to ecumenism is one sign of a renewed commitment to diversity, are there other areas where a similar reclamation of this key liberal theological principle is needed today? There seem to me to be four which particularly demand attention: the diversity within the major faith traditions and their scriptures; sexual diversity; biodiversity; and attitudes to other faiths and cultures.

Of all the remarks made at the Scottish Inter-Faith Day that I had the privilege of chairing on St Andrew's Day 2008, the one that struck me most was made by Imam Muhammad Ashafa: 'The great need now is to rediscover the theology of diversity within our faith traditions.' The fact that this came from the principal Muslim speaker at the gathering was particularly significant, for it is perhaps Islam more than any other faith that needs to re-discover and acknowledge the diversity within its own tradition. The more open and mystical Sufi strain is in particular danger of being suffocated by the rise of narrow fundamentalism. As we have seen, the Koran makes much of the God-given nature of diversity, but increasingly monochrome and literalist readings mean that this perspective is being lost. They are wholly out of keeping with the great Muslim tradition of *itijihad* and wrestling for truth through dialogue, learning and independent reasoning. Several liberal Islamic scholars have recently argued that interpretative diversity is one of the hallmarks of the Islamic tradition, but they agree that it is currently in abeyance or decline and have called for a recovery of *itijihad* and the idea of reasoned, critical interpretation of both the Koran and shar'a.[24] Voices within Judaism are also calling for a return to the broad, imaginative process of interpretation to bridge the gap between the time when the Torah was written and the contemporary world which was introduced by the rabbis but is now in retreat in favour of a more literalist monochrome approach. One prominent Jewish scholar has recently written:

> God's fingerprints are all over the Torah. But so are those of our ancestors who wrote it down. It contains much that is Godly, but quite a bit that is all too human as well . . . The challenge that Judaism and Christianity must face is to reaffirm the divine fingerprints on Torah and New Testament, while acknowledging that which is time-bound, flawed, and even disgraceful and dangerous.[25]

Christianity, too, is suffering from an increasingly literalist and narrow interpretation of its scriptures at a time when biblical scholars, even of a relatively conservative hue, are increasingly pointing to the huge diversity of the Bible in terms of authorship, context, theology and interpretation. Virtually no one now regards the Pentateuch, the first five books of the Hebrew Bible and Christian Old Testament, as having been written by a single author. Indeed, one does not have to read any further than the first two chapters of Genesis to be confronted with two radically different accounts of the creation of the world. Scholars are virtually all agreed that the opening book of the Bible is a compilation of at least three separate Israelite traditions with markedly different origins, settings and perspectives. Reflecting on the consequence of reading Genesis in the light of this knowledge and as a compilation of different traditions rather than as a flat story with a single author and point of view, as it was long regarded before the modern era of biblical criticism, Theodore Hiebert writes:

> Genesis does not present us with a single theological or ethical perspective; rather, it contains multiple perspectives from Israelite life and experience. This fact itself is a theological issue, since it raises the question whether theological and ethical reflection is best served by a single honored point of view or by multiple voices with different perspectives that have gained respect.[26]

What Hiebert says of Genesis is true of many other books in the Bible. The theological diversity found in the Old Testament, which moves from primitive polytheism to ethical monotheism, is echoed in the New Testament with the divergent experiences of the Gospel writers and the widely different Christologies of John and Paul. In the words of the contemporary New Testament scholar David Aune: 'The New Testament is both the earliest witness to Christian theological diversity and a prime source for that diversity throughout the long history of Christianity.' He notes that the application of historical criticism has revealed that 'first-century Christian communities exhibited no greater a degree of theological unity than do the theological traditions of modern Christian denominations'.[27] Given the degree of diversity and ambiguity in the biblical texts, it follows that there must be widely differing interpretations of their meaning. As Keith Ward remarks, 'The besetting sin of Biblical interpretation is the failure to accept that there exist many diverse interpretations of the text. There is no "one true" understanding.'[28]

Just as important as acknowledging the diversity of the scriptures and their interpretation is recognizing and living with the wide diversity of theological and ethical views that co-exist within the Christian faith community and within individual churches. This is what many conservative evangelicals are now refusing to do in their drive to establish and enforce a single view (their own) on highly contentious issues. Addressing an Anglican gathering in 1991, Robert Runcie presciently observed that 'these may be days to concentrate less on increasing refinement and more on preservation of varieties in theology . . . Truth is many sided. Only a church which can comprehend diversity can believe in the development and unfolding of God's truth.'[29] Sadly, in Anglicanism as in other denominations, the trend has gone in the opposite direction, with uniformity being prized above diversity, as in the 2004 Windsor Report, commissioned in response to the widespread divergence of views within the Anglican communion on the subject of ordaining homosexuals. Reflecting on this report, Andrew Linzey observes, 'It is frequently accepted as axiomatic within Christian churches that uniformity of opinion on moral issues is desirable. But why? The strongest argument is that the Church should possess "the mind of Christ" and therefore be of one opinion. But the mistake here is to suppose that "the mind of Christ" is monochromatic and that correspondingly there is one view of every moral issue that our Lord wishes for each individual Christian, or for the whole church.' He points out how false this urge is to the actual character of Jesus portrayed in the Gospels as someone reluctant to give simple answers and preferring to throw out questions. As Linzey says, 'The fact is that there is a diversity of opinion on every moral issue of any importance confronting the Church today.' On certain highly contentious matters, such as whether or not the Church should endorse the maintenance of nuclear weapons, this diversity is accepted, while on others it is not. He rightly comments, 'It really will not do for some Christians to speak as though there is a legitimate diversity of view on questions such as the use of nuclear weapons, but a "line" that must be followed on such issues as capital punishment, divorce, abortion and homosexuality.'[30]

It is over the issue of homosexuality more than any other that militant conservative evangelicalism has eroded the commitment to breadth and diversity that has traditionally characterized mainstream Protestant churches and especially the national established churches of England and Scotland. I have already written about the hardening of policy in the Church of Scotland with regard to the blessing of same-sex civil partnerships which undermines the long tradition of ministerial freedom of conscience and pastoral discretion. Instead of a situation of diversity there is now a uniform, monochrome ruling according to the narrow lines drawn up by evangelicals. This is not just a blow for the liberal position on faithful, same-sex relationships, it is also a blow for the diversity, tolerance and respect for different views that has long characterized Scotland's national church. The General Assembly of the United Reformed Church took the brave and commendable decision in 2007 not to take a single line on the issues around homosexuality but to live with the profound differences of attitude and approach among its members. Resolving to live together with difference is not an easy option, as Clare Herbert points out in reflecting on her time as Rector of St Anne's Soho, an exceptionally diverse community, but it is surely what churches and faith communities are called to do by the God of diversity:

> In this living with difference we experience the odd moment of romance and sentimentality but more usually we get to know great difficulty. The one who is very different from me creates the gap, the absence, the wound, showing me that diversity is not the byword for a comfortable life but a real hard-edged place to be, of jarring and struggle and forgiveness, as we inch our way towards the wholeness in complexity for which we are made.[31]

For liberals, the issue of homosexuality is approached through a theological commitment to diversity as well as through grace, love and generous acceptance (page 68). Liberals maintain that homosexuality is not an aberration, a disease or a wilful, sinful deviation but a genetically conditioned part of the natural order of creation and evolution. Faithful and loving same-sex relationships should be blessed and affirmed for the same reason that heterosexual ones are, namely that 'those who dwell in love are dwelling in God, and God in them' (1 John 4.16). There is no intrinsic reason why gay people should not be ordained to ministry. The few biblical texts which seem to condemn homosexual behaviour have a very specific historical context and there is considerable debate among scholars as to their precise meaning and interpretation. Leviticus 18.22 and 20.13, two of the verses most frequently cited to justify Christian homophobia, are taken by many Old Testament scholars to refer specifically to homosexual rape and the breaking of hospitality laws, as are the less than explicit suggestions in Genesis that the sin of Sodom may have centred on homosexual acts. They stand alongside other culturally specific passages which have been used over the centuries to justify such practices as slavery, the beating of children and the burning of supposed witches. Paul's condemnation of homosexuality in Romans 1.26–27 seems to be directed primarily at heterosexuals who freely choose to act contrary to their natural inclinations. He may well have specifically had in mind the practices of male prostitution and pederasty which many New Testament scholars now regard as also being the targets of the condemnatory remarks in 1 Corinthians 6.9–10 and 1 Timothy 1.9–10. It is surely significant that Jesus is not once portrayed in the Gospels as asking about anyone's sexuality. His apparent indifference as to the sexual orientation of those whom he encountered stands in marked contrast to his concern about the way they used their money, their hypocrisy and their slavery to narrow legalism.

Liberals will have to keep on explaining and expounding the gospel of grace and proclaiming the God of diversity as long as conservative evangelicals oppose the ordination of gays and the blessing of same-sex partnerships. Instead of clinging to homophobic prejudices when almost everyone else in the Western world has abandoned them and spreading narrow negativity and fear, the churches should rejoice in sexual diversity and in relationships which are life affirming and loving. It seems a bizarre issue to be expending so much time and energy on when there are so many more important and pressing matters where the Church's prophetic witness and pastoral touch are desperately needed. Climate change, environmental degradation and the so-called 'clash of civilizations' between Christians, Jews and Muslims are much more important matters, although one would not think so from the obsession shared by the media and conservative evangelicals with issues around sexuality. It is these real and serious threats to the future of our planet and the human race that demand the attention and action of all of us, liberals and non-liberals alike.

Liberal Christianity has always been intrinsically sympathetic to what we now call environmentalism and the green agenda because of its emphasis on natural theology, its sense that God is to be found in creation as much as in revelation and its generally positive attitude to the physical world. However, even liberals have not been immune from the rampant anthropocentrism and dualism that has bedevilled Western theology. The essentially green message contained in the Bible, and found often even more explicitly in the sacred texts of other faiths, needs to be reclaimed and vigorously proclaimed. It is the message that God is concerned with and rejoices in creation in all its diversity and fullness, and that as humans we are called to be stewards and co-creators of this delicate, fragile, inter-dependent eco-system, to limit and restrain our greedy appetites and to live in a more ordered and mindful way. Care and respect for bio-diversity needs to be more integrated into our liturgies as well as into our lives through simpler, more sustainable living in the spirit of Samuel Taylor Coleridge's 'Rhyme of the Ancient Mariner':

> He prayeth well, who loveth well
> Both man and bird and beast.
> He prayeth best, who loveth best
> All things both great and small;
> For the dear God who loveth us,
> He made and loveth all.[32]

Although climate change is almost certainly the greatest threat that we currently face, the so-called 'clash of civilizations' manifested in the increasing friction between faiths, and especially between the three Abrahamic faiths of Judaism, Christianity and Islam, runs it a close second. This clash will be averted if the leaders of these faiths can recover their liberal heart and persuade their followers to espouse the ways of pluralism and respect for the other and the stranger so clearly extolled in their sacred scriptures. From his own Jewish perspective, Jonathan Sacks has led the way with his book *The Dignity of Difference* from which I am quoting so much in this chapter. The need for a similarly open espousal of religious and cultural diversity is particularly urgent in Islam. William Montgomery Watt observed over twenty years ago that:

One of the things that should now specially concern Muslims is a study of other religions in order to see what is a positive value in them. This is one facet of the most important change which is needed in the outlook of Muslims, namely an openness to all historical truth. Islamic thought lost its flexibility after the fourth Islamic century and became petrified, and this was largely because the historians allowed themselves to be dictated to by the needs of theological dogma.[33]

There is, in fact, a strong tradition of respect for religious pluralism in Islam. The Turkish scholar Ali Bulaç has persuasively argued that the Medina Document, by which the Prophet Muhammad granted complete autonomy in matters of religion, culture, education, health and other areas to non-Muslims, predominantly Jews and polytheists, living under Muslim rule, provides a model for respecting the rights of religious minorities. It is particularly important that the Sufi mystical tradition is reaffirmed with its conviction, expressed by the thirteenth-century Muslim writer, Jalaludin Rumi, that 'the lamps are different but the Light is the same: it comes from Beyond'.[34]

Liberal Christianity has a key contribution to make towards averting the 'clash of civilizations' by promoting religious and cultural pluralism and breaking down the barriers of distrust and suspicion of the other which are piling up around the fortresses of fundamentalism. Liberal Christians have long been in the vanguard of pushing the boundaries with regard to Christian understanding of other faiths. They pioneered the inclusivist approach, and more recently they have been prominent in developing the more radical pluralistic approach which sees other religions as authentic pathways to God and authentic ways of salvation or liberation on their own terms. John Hick, who moved in his own Christian pilgrimage from conservative evangelicalism to liberalism, is often taken to be the founding father of pluralism with his call in 1973 for a Copernican revolution in Christian theology, 'a shift from the dogma that Christianity is at the centre to the realisation that it is God who is at the centre and that all religions . . . including our own, serve and revolve around Him'.[35] Liberal Christians are likely to be either inclusivists, seeing some truth in all major faiths but feeling that they are incomplete and that Christianity represents their fulfilment, or pluralists, believing that all major religions are equally valid paths to God and that no single one can claim the final and definitive truth. Conservative evangelicals generally adhere to the exclusivist position that only one single revelation is true and all religions other than Christianity are false.

An important aspect of the liberal approach, whether inclusive or pluralist, is acknowledgement of the truths and insights found in the scriptures of other faiths and respect for their own traditions of exegesis. There is a particularly important issue of respect in terms of Christian attitudes towards Jewish interpretations of the Old Testament. Christianity is unique among major world religions in incorporating the scriptures of another faith into its own sacred canon. Within the overall context of anti-semitism, there has been a shameful history of the Christian churches claiming to be the sole valid interpreters of the Hebrew Bible and ignoring or despising Jewish exegesis. Recent pronouncements from the Roman Catholic Church have thankfully and at last heralded an end to this imperialistic practice and have acknowledged the validity of Jewish exegesis, its faithfulness to God's revelation and the fact that for Jews what Christians regard as the Old Testament constitutes a full and sufficient scriptural basis of faith. In another important and welcome development, liberal believers are finding new insights and a broadening of their faith by reading in parallel and sometimes in company with those of other religions the sacred texts of different traditions. I myself have benefited considerably from reading both on my own and in groups parallel passages from the Psalms, the Gospels, the Koran and the Upanishads. Fundamentalists will dismiss this as syncretism, but as those who have tried such an approach will testify, it is an experience that broadens and deepens rather than dilutes faith. For me as a Christian, Jesus remains the supreme incarnation and expression of God and the Way, the Truth and the Life but, as William Sloane Coffin observed, 'To say that God is defined by Christ is not to say that God is confined to Christ.'

In what is one of the most exciting and important developments in contemporary liberal theology, scholars from a variety of faith backgrounds are wrestling with the implications of religious diversity in terms of God's intention and call to humanity today. The Jesuit theologian, Jacques Dupuis, develops his Christian theology of religious pluralism on the basis of the Trinitarian God's grace-filled self-manifestation to human beings:

> The divine plan for humanity is one but multifaceted. It belongs to the nature of the overflowing communication of the Triune God to humankind to prolong outside the divine life the plural communication intrinsic to that life itself. That God spoke 'in many and various ways' before speaking through his Son is not incidental; nor is the plural character of God's self-manifestation merely a thing of the past. For the decisiveness of the Son's advent in the flesh in Jesus Christ does not cancel the universal presence and action of the Word and the Spirit. Religious pluralism in principle rests on the immensity of a God who is love.[36]

His Christian case for a theology of religious pluralism echoes Chief Rabbi Sacks' conviction that God is bigger than religion:

> God is universal, religions are particular. Religion is the translation of God into a particular language and thus into the life of a group, and Nation, a community of faith. In the course of history, God has spoken to mankind in many languages: through Judaism to Jews, Christianity to Christians, Islam to Muslims. Any such a God is truly transcendental – greater not only than the natural universe but also than the spiritual universe articulated in any single faith, any specific language of human sensibility. How could a sacred text convey such an idea? It would declare that *God is God of all humanity, but no single faith is or should be the faith of all humanity*. Only such a narrative would lead us to see the presence of God in people of other faiths. Only such a world view could reconcile the particularity of cultures with the universality of the human condition.[37]

These and other similar arguments being put forward by contemporary theologians naturally lead on to the ethical imperative to befriend the stranger and get alongside the other, in keeping with the repeated injunctions of the Hebrew Bible and the example of Jesus. As Marjorie Suchochi writes:

It is time for Christians to cease viewing persons from other religions as candidates for conversion. Rather they are potential
partners for conversation. Friendship, not competition, should be
our goal. Friends talk with each other, argue with each other, even
critique each other, but the underlying friendship means that
respect and caring underlie all forms of conversation. To disagree
with the other is not to disparage the other, but to engage each
other at the depth levels of who we are. In such dialogue, we have
much to learn not only about the other but about ourselves, and
about the God we love and serve. It may even be that just as we
delight in the differences represented in personal friendships, we
shall begin to delight in the creative differences represented in
interreligious friendships.

God is creator, ever creating. Let us honour God in honouring
the work of creation. Let us delight in the manyness of things and
the manyness of people.[38]

Friendship across faith boundaries of the kind advocated here is being
put into practice by liberal believers, and others, in many ways –
through work with asylum seekers and refugees, joint action on peace
and social justice issues, in women's aid groups, refuges and community
centres as well as through simple, straightforward hospitality and
sharing stories. It reflects the move that is taking place in inter-faith
encounter from tolerance to respect and then beyond respect to friendship and sharing. It is often personal rather than institutional, and
much of the most important work is being done by women and is
highly practical. The pioneer historian and advocate of the study of
comparative religion, William Cantwell Smith, very sensibly remarked
that 'no one should have any views on interreligious questions until he
or she has talked with members of other communities; and preferably,
not until he or she has friends among them'.[39] On this friendship model,
inter-faith encounter becomes love in action as people meet, eat
together, listen to each other's stories, form relationships and co-
operate in practical projects. They do not seek to convert one another
or find unity, still less uniformity, but rather to walk together as
pilgrims, not strangers.

None of this is easy and it demands a choice. In this chapter I have tended to quote those passages in the scriptures of the three monotheistic faiths that emphasize diversity and pluralism, kinship with the stranger and reaching out to the other. There are plenty of other texts that I could have quoted which go in the opposite direction, restricting the divine relationship to one chosen people and one faith and encouraging narrow particularism, suspicion of strangers, and intolerance toward those of different beliefs. It is these harsh and ungracious texts, more often than not born out of situations of fear and conflict, which are taken up by fundamentalists and used as a justification for bigotry, intolerance and, in the worst cases, for acts of terrorism and genocide. As Sacks writes, 'The choice is ours. Will the generous texts of our tradition serve as interpretive keys to the rest, or will the abrasive passages determine our ideas of what we are and what we are called on to do?'[40] Liberals can have no doubt as to what their choice must be in an increasingly dangerous world: reclaiming the gracious, open embrace of diversity that is at the heart of the three great monotheistic faiths and taking the fundamentalists head on.

> Fundamentalism, like imperialism, is the attempt to impose a single truth on a plural world. It is the Tower of Babel of our time.
>
> The test of faith is whether I can make space for difference. Can I recognise God's image in someone who is not in my image, whose language, faith, ideals, are different from mine? If I cannot, then I have made God in my image instead of allowing him to remake me in his. Can Israeli make space for Palestinian, and Palestinian for Israeli? Can Muslims, Hindus, Sikhs, Confucians, Orthodox, Catholics and Protestants make space for one another in India, Sri Lanka, Chechnya, Kosovo and the dozens of other places in which different ethnic and religious groups exist in close proximity? Can we create a paradigm shift through which we come to recognise that we are enlarged not diminished by difference?[41]

The task to which I, like Jonathan Sacks, believe that God is now calling all of us, to see in the human other a reflection of the divine other and to embrace difference and diversity, is far from easy. For Christians, with their Trinitarian perspective, it has a special imperative because of God's own diversity, Jesus' particular outreach to the other and the way that he comes to us, in Albert Schweitzer's famous words, 'as One unknown'. We are especially enjoined to make the first move and walk the extra mile. Embracing diversity takes us to the heart of liberal faith, with its gracious openness, its conviction of the conditionality and partiality of all human truth claims and of the ongoing, progressive nature of revelation. Liberals are naturally eirenic and seek common ground and overlapping identity, while respecting and indeed relishing variety and difference. They value the otherness of the other and believe that engaging with different perspectives and expressions of belief can deepen and affirm their own faith and identity rather than threaten it. In keeping with the hymnodic thread woven through this book, I end this chapter with a contemporary hymn to the God of diversity written by Andrew Pratt after reading the story of Jacob, Laban, Leah and Rachel in Genesis 29.

O Source of many cultures,
Of lives, beliefs and faith;
You brought us all together
To share one world in space;
Now show us how to honour
Each vision of your way,
To live within the tension
Of difference you display.

The colour and the culture,
That kept us both apart,
Are gifts that we can offer,
A means for us to start
A journey with each other;
Till hand in hand we show,
Through mutual understanding,
Respect and love can grow.[42]

Notes

1. Skorupski 2006, p. 53.
2. N. D. O'Donoghue, 'St Patrick's Breastplate' in J. Mackey (ed.) *An Introduction to Celtic Christianity* (Edinburgh: T & T Clark, 1989), p. 46.
3. 'The Jordan, The Tiber and the Ganges' in Hick and Knitter 1988, p. 110.
4. Suchochi 2003, p. 66.
5. Boff 1988, p. 149.
6. M. Grey, *Introducing Feminist Images of God* (Sheffield: Sheffield Academic Press, 2001) p. 115.
7. Lecture, St Andrew's University, 2 July 2003.
8. C. Gunton, *The One, the Three, the Many* (Cambridge: Cambridge University Press, 1993), p. 7.
9. *Summa Theologiae*, Ia, 47.1. This translation is from T. Gilby (ed.), *St Thomas Aquinas Theological Texts* (London: Oxford University Press, 1955), p. 85.
10. On this point, see Bradley 1990, p. 32. For a scholarly attempt to construct a modern environmental ethic on Aquinas' work, see W. Jenkins, 'Biodiversity and Salvation: Thomistic Roots for Environmental Ethics', *Journal of Religion*, 83, No. 3 (July 2003), pp. 401–20.
11. 'A Telling Reminder of our Enduring Captivity to Myth', *Guardian*, 26 November 2008, p. 34.
12. Sacks 2002, p. 53.
13. 'The Tower of Babel and the Origin of the World's Cultures', *Journal of Biblical Literature*, Spring 2007, pp. 29–58. See also J. Dart, 'Is the Tower of Babel Wobbling?', *Christian Century*, 7 August 2007, and Hiebert's chapter on Genesis in O'Day and Petersen 2009, p. 16.
14. Sacks 2002, p. 54.
15. Sacks 2002, p. 56.
16. J. Danielou, *Holy Pagans in the Old Testament* (London: Longmans, Green, 1957). See also Dupuis 2002, pp. 34–40.
17. James Gregory Lecture, St Andrew's University.
18. R. L. Nettleship, *The Works of T. H. Green* (London: Longmans, Green, 1888), III, 240–1.
19. G. Matheson, *The Distinctive Messages of the Old Religions* (Edinburgh: Blackwood, 1892), p. 341.
20. G. Matheson, *Sacred Songs* (Edinburgh: William Blackwood, 3rd edn, 1904), pp. 36–8.
21. A. Carmichael, *Carmina Gadelica* (Edinburgh: Oliver & Boyd, 1928), I, 39.
22. Letter to *Guardian*, 29 September 2008, p. 35.
23. See Bradley 1992, pp. 47–8.

24. Kurzman 1998.
25. T. Bayfield, 'Time to Confront the Literalists', *Church Times*, 2 January 2009, p. 11.
26. 'Genesis' in G. O'Day and D. Petersen 2009, p. 4.
27. D. E. Aune, 'The New Testament: Source of Modern Theological Diversity', *Direction*, Vol. 2, No. 1 (January 1973), pp. 10–15.
28. Alker 2008, p. 34.
29. Lecture to Scottish Episcopal Church, 1 September 1991. I owe this reference to Peter Francis.
30. A. Linzey, *Has Anglicanism a Future?* (London: LGCM, 2005), pp. 12–13.
31. Alker 2008, p. 84.
32. Bradley 1990, *passim*.
33. W. M. Watt, *Islamic Fundamentalism and Modernity* (London: Routledge, 1988), p. 141.
34. 'The Medina Document', Kurzman 1998, pp. 169–78; *Rumi, Poet and Mystic*, trans. R. A. Nicholson (London: Allen & Unwin, 1950), p. 166.
35. J. Hick, *God and the Universe of Faiths* (London: Collins Fount, 1977), p. 131.
36. Dupuis 2002, p. 387.
37. Sacks 2002, p. 55.
38. Suchochi 2003, p. 35.
39. W. C. Smith, 'Christian–Muslim Relations: The Theological Dimension', *Studies in Interreligious Dialogue* (1991), Vol. 1, p. 8.
40. Sacks 2002, pp. 207–8.
41. Sacks 2002, p. 201.
42. Pratt 2002, p. 74. Reproduced by permission of Stainer & Bell Ltd, 23 Gruneisen Road, London N3 1DZ, www.stainer.co.uk.

7

Escaping from Fundamentalism and Living in God's Hope

This book has suggested ways to emerge from the long shadow cast by religious fundamentalism over the last hundred years and reclaim the liberal theology that lies at the heart of all the great faith traditions. I have identified this liberal theological tradition, which is found in the scriptures and sacred texts of all the major faiths and was often to the fore in their foundational stages before being overlaid with conservative reaction and fear, in terms of the four values of grace, order, openness and diversity. I have further suggested that these may also be taken as the central attributes of God, and for Christians as key characteristics of the three persons of the Trinity and of God in Trinity as a whole.

The four themes that I have highlighted are not to be taken in isolation nor as discrete and self-sufficient attributes either of liberal theology or of God. They overlap and interpenetrate one another and they need to be balanced by other values, as I hope I have acknowledged: grace by judgement, order by freedom, openness by dependability and faithfulness, diversity by unity. Conservatives can, indeed, help liberals achieve this balance, but it is because I believe the pendulum has swung too far in the conservative direction that I have felt the need particularly to highlight those liberal values and to urge their reclamation.

I hope that readers will not go away from this book feeling that I am seeking to present God or Jesus Christ as liberals in a narrow, partisan sense. I have already written a book entitled *God is Green* to emphasize the deep concern for creation and what we now call environmentalism that runs through the Christian scriptures. God is infinitely wider and bigger than any one theological tradition. I was never remotely tempted to entitle this book *God is Liberal* – that would be plain wrong as well as idolatrous – but I do believe that God is liberal in terms of the breadth, openness, diversity and wideness of God's mercy. Perhaps liberality is a better word to use – and as Peter Hodgson observes, 'Confidence in the gracious liberality of God means that we can and should be open to wherever the marks of this liberality are displayed in nature, culture and history.'[1] It would be equally wrong to label Jesus a liberal, but he is undoubtedly a liberator, calling and bringing people to life in all its fullness, teaching in an open-ended way and constantly putting love before the letter of the law.

One question has nagged at me throughout the writing of this book and needs to be addressed before it is finished. It is whether liberalism is the creed of the comfortable, living in pleasant circumstances and times. This is an accusation that is frequently levelled at political liberals, and something similar is often said of theological liberals. P. T. Forsyth observed that 'those who so speak seem never themselves to have resisted unto blood stirring against sin, nor to have been snatched from self-contempt and despair'.[2] The implication is that liberals are naive optimists who live on the surface and have never really plumbed the depths of human experience.

I think there is a measure of truth in this. In my own experience, many liberals have had a secure, safe upbringing and live in relative comfort. By contrast, conservative evangelicalism often appeals, especially through its characteristic entry point of instant conversion, to those with disturbed and unhappy backgrounds or coming out of a dark tunnel of abuse, depression or addiction. Most theological liberals that I know have grown up in the faith and not undergone a radical conversion experience, although there is also a growing number who have made the journey from conservative evangelicalism. This lack of a dramatic conversion or born-again event is something that liberals can be made to feel bad about by conservative evangelicals who seem to see us as second-class citizens because faith has always been part of our lives and experience.

There does seem to be a real point of difference here between the make-up and background of many liberal and conservative believers. I highlighted it in the book I wrote nearly twenty years ago about the state of Christianity in Britain which distinguished what I called the visible and invisible churches, the former being the mainstream broadly

liberal traditional denominations meeting in recognizable church build-
ings with spires and stained-glass windows, and the latter the new
evangelical house churches and fellowships meeting in school and
community halls.

> It seems to me that what I have described as the visible and the
> invisible churches speak to and cater for two entirely different
> groups in society. The first is made up of those whose lives are
> largely ordered and without major upsets, who have themselves
> probably been brought up with Christian values and in stable
> homes. The other consists of those whose lives have been fractured,
> dislocated and disorderly, who have often come to Christianity
> from outside, and sometimes after dabbling in the occult, witch-
> craft or drugs. I suspect that there are also significant psychological
> and theological differences between the followers of the two kinds
> of church. The visible church tends to attract those who see them-
> selves going on steadily in their faith, growing gradually in it,
> sometimes falling back a bit. The invisible church, by contrast,
> appeals to those who have a much more dramatic sense of conver-
> sion and of making the decision to follow Christ, and a much
> greater assurance of their personal salvation.[3]

Although there are encouraging signs of a greater theological openness
and pilgrim sense developing in the new house churches and fellowships and within the whole emerging church movement, there still
seems to me to be much truth in that observation. Different life experiences and personality types tend to be attracted to and to shape liberal
and conservative theology. It is almost as if the differences between
liberals and conservatives are genetically programmed. These differences are to be welcomed. A world populated only by liberals would be
monochrome and lack the diversity that I have suggested is an essential
attribute of God and God's creation. Conservatives constantly challenge and prompt those of us who are liberals to work out and articulate what it is that we believe. If I were not surrounded by them, I
would never have written this book!

There is another, more serious way in which liberals need conservative challenge and criticism. It takes us back to the accusation that

liberalism is essentially a creed for the comfortable. Continuing his critique quoted above, P. T. Forsyth wrote that liberals need to grow into a less superficial, optimistic relationship with God. In his words, 'our sunny liberalism' must pass 'from a trout stream of the morning to the river of God which is full of deep water'.[4] I can see what he means. I am not sure that liberals need to take on the 'self-contempt and despair' that he writes about and adopt the grovelling self-chastisement of Newton and Watts (see pages 50–1). However, he is quite right to suggest that those of us who are liberals can dwell rather too much in the sunny, shallow, calm of the trout pool and not venture into darker and deeper waters. For all their attachment to reason and order, liberals need to engage with the mystics, to have a sense of the holiness as well as of the grace of God, and to acknowledge that 'the fear of the Lord is the beginning of wisdom'. We need, too, to recognize the reality and power of sin, evil and human depravity. Liberal believers, just like conservative believers, are called to repentance, humility and silence, as well as to righteous indignation and action, in the face of the dark side of the world and of human nature and in the face of the awesome mystery of God.

It is also true that in more general terms liberalism tends to thrive in settled and ordered times rather than in situations of disruption and distress. Alistair Mason rightly observes in his entry on liberal Protestantism in the *Oxford Companion to Christian Thought*, 'liberalism prospers in peaceful, stable societies with some economic growth, where progress is sensible hope'.[5] It is no coincidence that both political and theological liberalism reached its apogee in the late nineteenth century, an age of exceptional stability, growing prosperity, and some would say, of complacency. Can liberalism flourish in the very unsettled and troubled atmosphere of the early twenty-first century? It is worth recalling that in the twentieth century, liberals were not just found among those enjoying comfortable and easy lives – Dietrich Bonhoeffer and the Confessing Church in Nazi Germany, and Trevor Huddleston and the opposition to Apartheid in South Africa are examples of liberal theological movements born out of profound discomfort and struggle. Liberalism has often manifested itself, if not always flourished, in difficult times. Indeed, it is not a particularly comfortable option to adopt in the present climate. Liberals who stick their heads above the parapet and express their views today are perhaps moving from Forsyth's 'trout stream of the morning to the river of God which is full of deep water'.

This raises the question of how far in coming out of their comfort zones and engaging with a profoundly illiberal world today, liberals should be more aggressive and less polite. It is a long-standing dilemma and a difficult one to resolve in the present climate. I find it very difficult to advocate that liberals should become graceless, even if we should be prepared to be bolder and stand our ground more, because that way seems to me to lead to a betrayal of what is at the heart of our being. Liberals surely cannot but maintain their gracious, generous witness to the God who is 'slow to chide and swift to bless' and does not weigh our merits but pardons our offences. This means adopting a constant patient attitude of blessing and affirmation in the face of intolerance and judgementalism.

Going around graciously blessing and affirming goodness may seem a rather vacuous and wishy-washy calling, epitomizing what our conservative critics and colleagues find so spineless and weak, but it is inescapably at the heart of the liberal temperament and it has its own toughness and rigour. For me, one of its finest recent exemplars was Robert Runcie, Archbishop of Canterbury from 1980 to 1990. During his period of office he came under considerable criticism, much of it very wounding, for being weak, indecisive and uncertain in his leadership. But, as his son wrote in a moving tribute shortly after his retirement, it is easy to see doubt where there is really ambivalence, indecision where there is forbearance, dithering and weakness where there is thought, pause and reflection. James Runcie admitted that he got so fed up with his father being pilloried in the press that he once implored him, 'Can't you do anything? Can't you be clearer, stronger?' The reply from his father was almost angry: 'I am strong on forgiveness and tolerance. I am clear in my faith in Jesus Christ. And I believe in authority – the authority of love.'[6]

Liberal graciousness and generosity do not equate with weakness. Liberals are called on to confront attitudes and institutions which threaten and diminish all that is created in God's image and which cramp the human personality and human creativity. We must take on the bullying of fundamentalists, but do so with the grace which is the hallmark not just of the liberal mind but also, insofar as we can discern it, of the mind of God, the One who speaks through the earthquake, wind and fire with the still, small voice. It will strike some as a very Quixotic enterprise, foolhardy, old-fashioned and perhaps even a touch élitist. It does, indeed, involve going back to those first definitions of the word 'liberal' to be found in the dictionary about being worthy of a free man or becoming of a gentleman. It is about cultivating character and emphasizing good behaviour rather than points of doctrine. It takes us back to those high-minded ethical imperatives of nineteenth- and early twentieth-century liberalism, to Harnack's emphasis on Jesus as the man for others and the model for us to follow, although it is worth noting that these are precisely the themes being championed by the most radical contemporary theologians, like Richard Holloway who argues that 'it is more important to follow the way of Jesus than to believe or disbelieve the traditional Christian claims about him'.[7] In an increasingly brutalized and uncouth world, it means displaying the 'good form, gentle faith, genial love and kindly conference' so carica-tured by Forsyth and other critics of the liberal position. It is in many ways an unglamorous and thankless calling – to be the still, small voice of calm in the maelstrom of noisy fundamentalist certainties and to be in for the long slog rather than the quick, spectacular result. As Alistair Mason expresses it, 'the liberal tradition goes on, seriously and subtly engaging with ethical questions, always wanting to express love and freedom and not the letter of the law'.[8]

There is, in fact, evidence that over recent years liberals have come out of the closet to take on conservatives and re-state their own position and commitment more clearly and boldly. In large measure this has happened in reaction to the rising tide of fundamentalism. In the more polarized and partisan atmosphere in which churches now find themselves, and where they are increasingly being split and divided along theological lines, thanks largely to conservative pressure to draw more distinct boundaries and jettison the traditional tolerance and breadth found in most mainstream denominations, liberals are having to come out and show their colours. As a result, long-standing liberal groups have undergone a new lease of life and new ones have been set up both in individual denominations and on a more ecumenical basis.

In Britain, the longest established such group is the predominantly Anglican Modern Churchpeople's Union, which traces its roots back well over 100 years. Its beginnings in 1898 as The Churchmen's Union for the Advancement of Liberal Religious Thought could be taken to mark the high-water mark of British liberal theology, although its formation also marked an acknowledgement of the need to defend new scientific findings – especially evolution – and biblical scholarship against the first stirrings of fundamentalism. It became known as the Modern Churchmen's Union in 1928 and assumed its present title in 1986. Explicitly committed to promoting liberal theology, it has recently undergone a new lease of life, publishing the journal *Modern Believing* and a lively newsletter *Signs of the Times* and running well-attended annual conferences. It has robustly criticized the Windsor Report for its illiberal tendencies and was the only major Christian group to lobby in favour of assisted dying when Lord Joffe's Bill came before Parliament. Describing itself as 'a mixed bunch of people who share an open-minded and thoughtful approach to Christian faith', its statement of belief reads as follows:

We believe that
- genuine faith is committed to the search for truth, wherever it comes from;
- God invites us to do our believing in ways appropriate to the twenty-first century;
- we never have absolute certainty; only God is infallible.

We appeal to a balance of scripture, tradition and reason, recognizing that all three sometimes err. If they did not, truth would be fixed in the past and we would have no potential for discovering anything new and exciting.

We believe in
- open discussion: freedom to explore ideas, ask questions and change our minds without fear of disapproval;
- critical scholarship: keeping up to date with good research, examining the implications of new insights and discoveries;
- willingness to change: so that what we believe now can be expressed in our doctrines, liturgies and ethics.

We expect our theology to be

- public: talking the language of ordinary people, not living apart in a religious club of its own;
- relevant: making links with what is going on in society, caring about current events and expecting our faith to contribute to our caring;
- respectful: willing to learn from others, within and outside Christianity, since we accept that we don't have all the answers.[9]

Other, more recently formed liberal pressure groups have sprung up within individual denominations as a direct reaction to the increasing mobilization of conservative evangelicalism. Free to Believe is a good example, founded in the United Reformed Church to counter the growing influence of the conservative Group for Evangelism and Renewal formed in 1974. Beginning with a conference entitled 'Free to Believe – Taking Our Liberal Past into the Future' held in Windermere in 1996 and organized by Martin Camroux and Donald Hilton 'to positively affirm the liberal heritage of the URC', it now has a mailing list of over 350 and its conferences regularly attract around 100 people. Free to Believe provides this statement of 'shared assumptions':

- That thinking seriously and critically strengthens rather than weakens faith – We believe that a healthy faith requires application of the intellect, not its abdication.

- That any religion which imagines it has a monopoly of truth is dangerous – claims of exclusive access to God can soon become demonic.

- That the ministry of Jesus sets an inclusive agenda for the Church – male and female, any culture and colour, straight and gay.

- That the Gospel is that God so loved the world, not that God so loved the Church – we have to stop retreating from the giant social issues of the day into the pygmy world of private piety.[10]

Even more recently established groups include One Kirk, set up in the Church of Scotland in 2006 to affirm the values of an inclusive, broad church in response to the mobilization of conservatives in a pressure group entitled Forward Together. One Kirk has been particularly concerned to expound the liberal position in the debates over the blessing of civil partnerships and the issue of homosexual clergy in the Church of Scotland. Affirming Liberalism, set up in the Diocese of Oxford in 2008, lists among its principal aims, 'reclaiming the use of the word "Liberal" in its Christian context, rescuing it from the negative prefix – woolly!' and 'encouraging Liberal Christians to be: confident not apologetic, visible not invisible, vocal not silent, overt not covert, free not fearful, strong not weak'. Specifically for those in the Liberal Anglican tradition, it has a tenfold statement of purpose:

1. Affirming faith in Jesus' life, teaching, death and resurrection as revealing God's limitless love for all humanity in this life and the next.
2. Affirming the dynamic action of God's Spirit in dispersing this divine love throughout the world.
3. Affirming the beneficial insights of biblical, literary and historical criticism for our understanding of Scripture and Tradition.
4. Affirming a free, questioning and philosophical approach to Christian faith through God-given reason.
5. Affirming the profound significance of science and mathematics in forming a Christian world-view and understanding of the universe.
6. Affirming the positive benefits of the social sciences for comprehending human nature and society, and in developing Christian ethics.
7. Affirming appreciation of the distinctive nature of religious language in vibrant worship which connects us to the divine.
8. Affirming the vitality of the performing and creative arts in shaping a dynamic Christian vision of life lived in relation to God.
9. Affirming open, creative conversation between Liberals, Evangelicals and Catholics as a means of enriching our understanding of the Christian gospel.
10. Affirming open, creative conversation with other faith traditions and cultures as a way of deepening our understanding of God.[11]

It is not just in the United Kingdom that theological liberals are at last coming out into the open, getting their act together and engaging in the kind of proselytizing usually associated with conservative evangelicals. Similar groups have also sprung up in the United States. Almost certainly the most significant is The Center for Progressive Christianity set up in 1996 by Jim Adams when he was rector of St Mark's Church on Capitol Hill in Washington DC and now a national movement with numerous affiliates and regional groupings. It has spawned a British offspring, the Progressive Christianity Network, which began unofficially in 2001, was officially launched in 2003 and now has over 35 local groups and over 4,000 members. The Progressive Christianity logo is an eight-pointed star reflecting the eight values that the movement espouses:

We are Christians who

- have found an approach to God through the life and teachings of Jesus;
- recognize the faithfulness of other people who have other names for the gateway to God's realm, and acknowledge that their ways are true for them, as our ways are true for us;
- understand the sharing of bread and wine in Jesus' name to be a representation of an ancient vision of God's feast for all peoples;
- invite all people to participate in our community and worship life without insisting that they become like us in order to be acceptable, including but not limited to: believers and agnostics, conventional Christians and questioning sceptics, women and men, those of all sexual orientations and gender identities, those of all races and cultures, those of all classes and abilities, those who hope for a better world and those who have lost hope;
- know that the way we behave toward one another and toward other people is the fullest expression of what we believe;
- find more grace in the search for understanding than we do in dogmatic certainty, more value in questioning than in absolutes;
- form ourselves into communities dedicated to equipping one another for the work we feel called to do: striving for peace and justice among all people; protecting and restoring the integrity

of all God's creation; and bringing hope to those Jesus called the least of his sisters and brothers;

- recognize that being followers of Jesus is costly, and entails selfless love, conscientious resistance to evil, and renunciation of privilege.[12]

Another significant recent American initiative is Living the Questions, a range of resources for the exploration of progressive Christianity originally designed by two United Methodist pastors for their congregations in Phoenix, Arizona. Its DVDs and on-line resources, which feature such liberal luminaries as John Dominic Crossan, Marcus Borg, John Spong, John Bell, Hans Kung and Walter Brueggemann, are now being used by over 5,000 churches and provide a liberal alternative to the ubiquitous Alpha course.

It is important not to over-exaggerate the impact being made by these liberal initiatives. They are considerably smaller than comparable conservative evangelical pressure groups and programmes but they are growing and they represent a significant advance on the situation just fifteen years or so ago when there were almost no liberal groups around. Their statements of belief represent a welcome, clear and accessible guide to current liberal theological thinking and counter the conservative criticism that liberals either do not know what they believe or do not believe in anything. Not surprisingly, they follow the traditional liberal preference for broad, open principles rather than the conservative demand for adherence to specific narrow doctrines. Ultimately, liberal theology is more about cultivating an attitude of mind and a way of behaving than drawing up declarations of belief, but the latter have their place and cannot be avoided in today's world of sound-bites and mission statements. For brevity and inclusivity, I cannot think of a better modern encapsulation of the essence of liberal theology than the object passed at the General Assembly of the Unitarian and Free Christian Churches in 2001: 'To promote a free and inquiring religion through the worship of God and the celebration of life; the service of humanity and respect for all creation; and the upholding of the liberal Christian tradition.'

It is too early to celebrate the turning of the modern fundamentalist tide that was unleashed 100 years ago with the publication of the pamphlets on the fundamentals of the faith. There are few signs of a revival of the great Islamic liberal tradition of *itijihad*, and Muslim fundamentalism still seems to be largely advancing unchecked. But Christian fundamentalism is increasingly being challenged, not least by many within the new emergent church movement, by charismatics open to the imaginative and experiential kind of faith championed by Schleiermacher, and by growing numbers of open and progressive evangelicals in both the United Kingdom and the United States. Maybe, just maybe, fundamentalism will indeed turn out to have been not just the great twentieth-century heresy but also the twentieth-century aberration.

Some of the most significant stirrings of this new renaissance of liberal theology are happening in a very unlikely place. In the early part of this book I located the origins of modern religious fundamentalism in the United States, and throughout it I have been especially critical of North American theological conservatism. It gives me considerable pleasure to end the book by pointing to a recent event in the United States, the presidential election of Barack Obama, which I believe may well provide a major boost to the cause of liberal theology globally in the twenty-first century.

Barack Obama is both an exemplar and an exponent of classic liberal theology. In the words of Stephen Mansfield, the author of a fascinating and revealing book about his faith, 'he is unapologetically Christian and unapologetically liberal'.[13] Obama was raised in a tradition of religious pluralism. Growing up in Indonesia in the late 1960s, he went to a Roman Catholic school, attended a mosque with his Muslim stepfather and imbibed an eclectic spiritual mix from his mother, herself raised as a Unitarian and determined to instil into her son her belief that underlying all great religions was a common set of ethical values and beliefs about how you treat other people. 'In our household', he has written, 'the Bible, the Koran and the Bhagavad Gita sat on the shelf alongside books of Greek and Norse and African mythology. On Easter or Christmas Day my mother might drag me to church, just as she dragged me to the Buddhist temple, the Chinese New Year celebration, the Shinto shrine and ancient Hawaiian burial sites.'[14]

Obama's journey to Christianity came through one of the most liberal denominations in the USA, the United Church of Christ, and specifically through a church that espoused black liberation theology and was pro-women and pro-gay. He made the decision to commit to Christianity after hearing a sermon on the audacity of hope by the Reverend Jeremiah Wright, pastor of Trinity United Church of Christ in Chicago in 1985. In his own words, 'It came about as a choice and not an epiphany; the questions I had did not magically disappear. But kneeling beneath that cross on the south side of Chicago, I felt God's spirit beckoning me. I submitted myself to his will, and dedicated myself to discovering his truth.'[15] The phrase about discovering God's truth shows that for Obama becoming a Christian did not involve closing his mind or shutting the door to further searching. He has written that his is 'a faith that admits doubt and uncertainty and mystery . . . In fact, it's not faith if you're absolutely certain. There's a leap that we all take and when you admit that doubt publicly, it's a form of testimony.' He admits that 'there are aspects of the Christian tradition that I'm comfortable with, aspects that I'm not. There are passages of the Bible that make perfect sense to me and others that I go "Ya know, I'm not sure about that".'[16]

Obama displays many of the key hallmarks of liberal Christianity as it has been described in this book. He has a very open attitude to other faiths, writing that 'I am rooted in the Christian tradition but I believe there are many paths to the same place and that is a belief that there is a higher power, a belief that we are connected as a people'. He rejects the notion of eternal punishment on the grounds that 'I find it hard to believe that my God would consign four-fifths of the world to hell.'[17] He supports civil unions for homosexuals and utterly rejects Christian anti-gay rhetoric, saying 'I am not willing to accept a reading of the Bible that considers an obscure line from Romans to be more defining of Christianity than the Sermon on Mount.'[18] He takes a pro-choice line on abortion but approaches this vexed question with a lack of dogmatic certainty, conceding that 'I cannot claim infallibility in my support of abortion rights.'[19] His focus is on Jesus as a real person to be imitated for his moral example rather than as a bearer of substitutionary atonement.[20] He does not view the Bible as a closed text and final statement and is open to continuing revelation: 'When I read the Bible, I do so with the belief that it is not a static text but the Living Word and that I must be continually open to new revelations – whether they come from a lesbian friend or a doctor opposed to abortion.'[21] He has a clear commitment to science and to scientific research, signalled by the pledge in his Inauguration Address, 'We will restore science to its rightful place', an implicit repudiation and rebuke of the previous President's flirtation with creationism and opposition to stem-cell research.

It may seem wildly fanciful to pin the prospects for the future of liberal theology on the election of a single politician, but Obama is the standard-bearer for a new theological and political liberalism that is emerging in the United States and challenging the hold of both the secular left and the religious right. The new religious left, as it has been called, embraces evangelicals like Jim Wallis, founder of the progressive Sojourners movement, who feel that conservative evangelicalism has focused excessively on narrow, negative campaigns like opposition to abortion and gay marriage, and ignored the much more important issues of social and economic justice and peace. Obama has given voice to this new emerging liberal movement which brings together progressive politics and progressive faith. He has reclaimed progressive liberal causes from being the monopoly of the secularists and challenged the notion that only the religious right have faith. As he said at the 2004 Democratic National Convention, 'Those of us who believe in a woman's right to choose an abortion, who defend the rights of our gay friends and who trust that big government can be a tool of righteousness, we also love God. We, too, have spiritual passion. No longer will we be painted as the non-believers. No longer will we yield the spiritual high ground. The Religious Right has nothing on us any more.'[22]

As I write this, Barack Obama has been in office for a year. He has been mercilessly attacked by the American right and although he has yet to deliver on all his liberal promises, there is still a feeling of a genuine new dawn in the United States. If the land that gave birth to modern fundamentalism and that has nurtured it for the last hundred years is, indeed, moving towards a new liberal faith, the consequences across the world could be considerable.

It is no coincidence that the sermon that inspired Barack Obama's espousal of liberal Christianity was on 'The Audacity of Hope', a phrase that he subsequently took as the title for his best-known and best-selling book and that has inspired his political career and presidency. The rhetoric of hope is fundamental to liberalism. I entitled my book about the mind and personalities of Victorian Liberalism *The*

Optimists. In the nineteenth century there was reason and room for optimism. In the early twenty-first century there are not many reasons for optimism understood, as it was in the Victorian age, as a belief in progress and all being for the best in the best of all possible times. We live with the reality of climate change, increasing poverty and inequality and heightening ethnic, racial and religious tensions. Optimism is not much use in this situation, but hope is essential – the hope that is born for Christians out of the cross of Christ and that Paul describes as the hope that is not seen (Romans 8.24). What we need now is not the shallow, comfortable optimism of the late nineteenth and early twentieth centuries that Forsyth caricatured as the 'sunny liberalism' of the trout stream of the morning, but a much more nuanced, reflective, engaged liberalism that flows in the deep water of the river of God but is still full of hope.

Hope is essential to the facing down of fundamentalism. At the moment we largely look on the future with fear as we contemplate climate change, the terrorist threat, increasing crime and social unrest. Fear is the climate in which fundamentalism flourishes and in which we become increasingly illiberal, de-personalized, box-ticking and untrusting. Faith, hope and charity all have a key place in the liberal theological pantheon, but of the three, hope is perhaps the greatest and most characteristic liberal virtue. It is not the same as naive optimism, it offers no easy solutions, it is vulnerable and humble, it can easily be squashed and frequently be misunderstood, but it is the most precious resource we have – and it comes from God, the God who affirms and builds us up, who is always ahead of us, luring us on and pointing to the future.

I want to end this book, as I have punctuated it, with one of the great hymns of liberal faith. I nearly chose Jan Struther's 'Lord of All Hopefulness' which celebrates and addresses God with a wonderful catalogue of liberal attributes as Lord of all joy, Lord of all eagerness, Lord of all faith, Lord of all kindliness, Lord of all grace, Lord of all gentleness and Lord of all calm. After much deliberation, however, I have decided to conclude with 'All My Hope on God is Founded', written by Robert Bridges (1844–1930) and loosely based on a German hymn by Joachim Neander (1650–80). This is because, as well as pointing to God's goodness, this hymn emphasizes our human dependence on God, for our hope as for everything else. It may seem odd to end a book about liberal theology on the theme of dependence, but I do not think it incongruous. That freest of all denominations from doctrine and dogma, the Society of Friends, emphasizes the importance of encouraging 'a habit of dependence on God's guidance for each day'.[23] Liberals, in common with all humanity, are creatures of God and utterly dependent on his wonderful bounty and grace. Love does stand at God's hand, and joy undoubtedly waits on his command.

> All my hope on God is founded;
> He doth still my trust renew,
> Me through change and chance He guideth,
> Only good and only true.
> God unknown, He alone
> Calls my heart to be His own.
>
> Pride of man and earthly glory,
> Sword and crown betray His trust;
> What with care and toil He buildeth,
> Tower and temple fall to dust.
> But God's power, hour by hour,
> Is my temple and my tower.
>
> God's great goodness aye endureth,
> Deep His wisdom, passing thought:
> Splendour, light and life attend Him,
> Beauty springeth out of naught.
> Evermore from His store
> Newborn worlds rise and adore.
>
> Daily doth th'almighty Giver
> Bounteous gifts on us bestow;
> His desire our soul delighteth,
> Pleasure leads us where we go.
> Love doth stand at His hand;
> Joy doth wait on His command.

Notes

1. P. Hodgson, 'Liberal Theology and Transformative Pedagogy' in Chapman 2002, p. 106.
2. P. T. Forsyth, *Positive Preaching and the Modern Mind* (Cincinatti: Jennings & Graham, 1907), p. 154.
3. Bradley 1992, p. 62.
4. Forysth, *Positive Preaching*, p. 154.
5. *Oxford Companion to Christian Thought*, p. 386.
6. Bradley 1992, pp. 220–1.
7. Holloway 2001, p. 18.
8. *Oxford Companion to Christian Thought*, p. 387.
9. www.modchurchunion.org.
10. http://freetobelieve.org.uk.
11. http://www.affirming-liberalism.org.uk/about/.
12. http://www.pcnbritain.org.uk/index.php/about/the_8_points/.
13. Mansfield 2008, p. xv.
14. Mansfield 2008, p. 55.
15. Mansfield 2008, p. 50.
16. Mansfield 2008, p. 54.
17. Mansfield 2008, p. 57.
18. Mansfield 2008, p. 57.
19. Mansfield 2008, p. 98.
20. On this see J. K. Wilson, *Barack Obama: This Improbable Quest* (Boulder: Paradigm, 2007), p. 136.
21. Mansfield 2008, p. 58.
22. Mansfield 2008, p. xv.
23. *Advice & Queries* (London: Society of Friends, 1997), p. 5.

Bibliography

A. Alker, *Together in Hope* (Sheffield: St Mark's CRC Press, 2008).

J. Bennett, *Reviving Liberty: Radical Christian Humanism in Milton's Great Poems* (Harvard: Harvard University Press, 1989).

J. C. Bivins, *Religion of Fear: The Politics of Horror in Conservative Evangelicalism* (New York: Oxford University Press, 2008).

L. Boff, *Trinity and Society* (Tunbridge Wells: Burns and Oates, 1988).

R. Boyd, *The Witness of the Student Christian Movement* (London: SPCK, 2007).

I. Bradley, *The Optimists: Themes and Personalities in Victorian Liberalism* (London: Faber & Faber, 1980).

——, *God is Green* (London: Darton, Longman & Todd, 1990).

——, *Marching to the Promised Land: Has the Church a Future?* (London: John Murray, 1992).

——, *The Power of Sacrifice* (London: Darton, Longman & Todd, 1995).

——, *Colonies of Heaven: Celtic Models for Today's Church* (London: Darton, Longman & Todd, 2000).

——, *Believing in Britain: The Spiritual Identity of Britishness* (Oxford: Lion Hudson, 2008).

——, *Pilgrimage – A Spiritual and Cultural Journey* (Oxford: Lion Hudson, 2009).

J. R. Carter (ed.), *Of Human Bondage and Divine Grace* (La Salle, Illinois: Open Court, 1992).

K. Cauthen, *The Impact of American Liberalism*, 2nd edn. (Washington: University Press of America, 1983).

M. D. Chapman (ed.), *The Future of Liberal Theology* (Aldershot: Ashgate, 2002).

J. Clatworthy, *Liberal Faith in a Divided Church* (Winchester: O Books, 2008).

J. Danielou, *Gospel Message and Hellenistic Culture*, trans. J. A. Baker (London: Darton, Longman & Todd, 1973).

G. Dorrien, *The Making of American Liberal Theology: Imagining Progressive Religion 1805–1900* (Louisville: Westminster John Knox Press, 2001).

——, *The Making of American Liberal Theology: Idealism, Realism and Modernity 1900–1950* (Louisville: Westminster John Knox Press, 2003).

——, *The Making of American Liberal Theology: Crisis, Irony and Post-modernity 1950–2005* (Louisville: Westminster John Knox Press, 2006).

J. Dupuis, *Towards A Christian Theology of Religious Pluralism* (London: Orbis, 2002).

H. A. R. Gibb, *Modern Trends in Islam* (Chicago: University of Chicago Press, 1947).

D. W. Hardy and P. Sedgwick (eds), *The Weight of Glory – A Vision and Practice for Christian Faith: The Future of Liberal Theology* (Edinburgh: T & T Clark, 1991).

S. Hauerwas, *Resident Aliens* (Nashville: Abingdon Press, 1989).

J. Hick and P. Knitter (eds), *The Myth of Christian Uniqueness* (London: SCM Press, 1988).

T. Hobson, *Milton* (London: Continuum, 2008).

R. Holloway, *Doubts and Loves: What is Left of Christianty* (Edinburgh: Canongate, 2001).

J. Jobling and I. Markham (eds), *Theological Liberalism* (London: SPCK, 2000).

J. Killinger, *Leave it to the Spirit* (London: SCM Press, 1971).

C. Kurzman (ed.), *Liberal Islam* (New York: Oxford University Press, 1998).

M. Langford, *A Liberal Theology for the Twenty-First Century: A Passion for Reason* (Aldershot: Ashgate, 2001).

G. Lindbeck, *The Nature of Doctrine: Religion and Theology in a Postliberal Age* (Philadelphia: Westminster Press, 1984).

S. Mansfield, *The Faith of Barack Obama* (Nashville: Thomas Nelson, 2008).

W. E. March, *The Wide, Wide Circle of Divine Love: A Biblical Case for Religious Diversity* (Louisville: Westminster John Knox Press, 2005).

E. Maroney, *Religious Syncretism* (London: SCM Press, 2006).

G. B. G. McConnell, *Memoirs of an Unrepentant Liberal* (privately published, 2001).

D. E. Miller, *The Case for Liberal Christianity* (London: SCM Press, 1981).

W. Montgomery Watt, *Islamic Fundamentalism and Modernity* (Routledge, 1988).

J. Morris (ed.), *To Build Christ's Kingdom: F. D. Maurice and His Writings* (London: Canterbury Press, 2007).

H. R. Niebuhr, *Christ and Culture* (New York: Harper, 1951).

G. O'Day and D. Petersen, *Theological Bible Commentary* (Louisville: Westminster John Knox Press, 2009).

D. Ottati, *Theology for Liberal Presbyterians and Other Endangered Species* (Louisville: Geneva Press, 2006).

A. Pratt, *Whatever Name or Creed* (London: Stainer & Bell, 2002).

F. Rahman, *Islam and Modernity: Transformation of an Intellectual Tradition* (Chicago: University of Chicago Press, 1982).

J. Rawls, *Lectures on the History of Political Philosophy* (Harvard University Press, 2007).

M. Richter, *The Politics of Conscience: T. H. Green and His Age* (London: Weidenfeld & Nicolson, 1964).

M. Ruthven, *Fundamentalism: The Search for Meaning* (Oxford: Oxford University Press, 2004).

J. Sacks, *The Dignity of Difference* (London: Continuum, 2002).

J. Skorupski, *Why Read Mill Today?* (Abingdon: Routledge, 2006).

M. Suchochi, *Divinity and Diversity: A Christian Affirmation of Religious Pluralism* (Nashville: Abingdon Press, 2003).

R. Warner *Reinventing English Evangelicalism, 1966–2001* (Milton Keynes: Paternoster, 2007).

J. Webster, *Theology After Liberalism* (Oxford: Blackwell, 2000).

D. Young, *F. D. Maurice and Unitarianism* (Oxford: Clarendon Press, 1992).

Index